Alfred's Teach Yourself To Sing

KAREN FARNUM SURMANI

PART I • THE SINGER WITHIN
Who Should Use This Book.................................... 2
Equipment 2
Practicing 3
Vocal Health 3
Acknowledgments 3
About the Recording 3
How to Read Music 4
The Symbols for Rhythm 6
Mini Music Lesson: Note-Reading Exercises 7

PART II • THE BASICS OF SINGING
Breathing 8
Physical Exercises 9
Vocalizing 10
Warming Up the Voice 10
Vowels 11
Oh, How Lovely Is the Evening 13
All Through the Night 13
Singing Posture 14
The Tongue 15
Mini Music Lesson: D.C. al Fine 16
All Night, All Day 16
Mini Music Lesson: Incomplete Measures 17
Home On the Range 17
The Jaw 18
Mini Music Lesson: Repeat Signs 19
Aura Lee 19
Kum Bah Yah 19
Singing Vowels and Consonants 20
Greensleeves 21
Long Time Ago 21
Matching Pitches 22
Merrily We Roll Along 23
Go, Tell It on the Mountain 23
Mini Music Lesson: The Fermata 24
Flow Gently, Sweet Afton 24
Are You Lonesome Tonight? 25
Mini Music Lesson: Cut Time 26
This Land Is Your Land 26

PART III • MORE BASICS OF SINGING
Vocal Space 27
The Water Is Wide 28
The Riddle Song 29
Energy 30
Mini Music Lesson: Ritardando, Poco rit., A tempo 31
Simple Gifts 31
Scarborough Fair 31
More Breathing Strategies 32
Drink to Me Only with Thine Eyes 33
The Band Played On 33
Vocal Resonance 34
Careless Love 35

Get on Board 35
Fear of Flying—or—Approaching "Higher" Pitches ... 36
Amazing Grace 38
Auld Lang Syne 39
Singing for Joy 40
Swing Low, Sweet Chariot 41
Water Come-A Me Eye 41
Choosing New Music 42
Learning Songs 42

PART IV • INTERPRETING VOCAL MUSIC
Give My Regards to Broadway 44
The Ash Grove 45
Musical Expression 46
Phrasing 46
Red River Valley 46
You Made Me Love You 47
Dynamics 48
Bye 'm Bye 49
Shenandoah 49
Legato and Staccato 50
Down in the Valley 51
Deck the Halls 51
Interpretive Exercises 52
Musical Styles 53
Popular Music 53
Jazz 53
Musical Theater 53
Classical Style 53
Putting It Together 53

PART V • PERFORMING MUSIC
Taking the Stage 54
Using a Microphone 55
Karaoke 55
A Few Last Words 55
Turn! Turn! Turn! 56
Those Were the Days 58
For All We Know 59
Fly Me to the Moon 60
Dream a Little Dream of Me 61
Where Is Love? 62
Now Is the Month of Maying 63
Chord and Scale Charts 64

Stream or download the media for this book. To access online media, visit: **www.alfred.com/redeem**
Enter the following code: 00-44769_882288

Alfred Music
P.O. Box 10003
Van Nuys, CA 91410-0003
alfred.com

Copyright © MMXV by Alfred Music
All rights reserved. Printed in USA.

ISBN-10: 1-4706-2972-0 (Book & Online Audio/Video/Software)
ISBN-13: 978-4706-2972-4 (Book & Online Audio/Video/Software)

Photo of Shure SM87 condenser microphone courtesy of Shure Brothers Inc. • Photo composite: Ted Engelbart, Phillip Oshiro • Diagrams: Christine Finn

 Alfred Cares. Contents printed on environmentally responsible paper.

GETTING
STARTED

PART I— THE SINGER WITHIN

The human voice has been used as a means of expression since the dawn of time. It is the oldest musical instrument. In all its forms, from wailing to whispering, speaking, shouting, singing, the purpose of the human voice is communication.

When we sing, we are communicating a message. Whether it is the message of a beautiful melody or a message contained in the words, the communication is ever present. It is the desire to communicate that spurs humans toward singing. The communication offered may be as simple as a happy feeling, or as complex as the meanings and symbolism contained in some poetry. Singing is a positive way of showing and venting emotions, but perhaps that is the very reason some people are apprehensive about the act of singing.

Now, for a startling truth—everyone has the ability to sing. The desire to sing resides in the human soul and spirit. If you have the desire, then yes, you can sing. Every person has a singer, a dancer, an artist inside them that is yearning to be granted the opportunity of expression. The goal of this book is to uncover your singer within and allow your song to be heard.

Singing is really a simple process, a matter of speaking on pitch, and trusting that our bodies know what to do. Even while knowing this to be true, many students of singing need to go through a re-education process in order to let go of any muscular tension in their singing so that they may fully achieve this state of simplicity and trust.

In search of their best singing voice, many students and amateur singers fail to realize their full potential because they are trying to sound like a certain singer or have a preconceived idea of how they should sound. They miss the point because the goal for each singer is to discover his or her own free, natural singing voice. Some voices may be characteristically "small" or "light," others "big" or "heavy." Trying to change an intrinsic part of one's voice will only lead to problems. A lily can't be changed into a rose, and why would anyone want it to be? Each flower has its own beauty. It is much the same when it comes to developing one's singing voice. The key is to take what we have and work to refine that.

Singers, as with any artists, cannot be free to develop their own abilities to the fullest while trying to emulate someone else. This is not to say that we can't learn from great singers, but we must realize that each person is unique, each with his or her own individual physiology and emotional makeup. These factors combine to produce a person's own exclusive sound. Of course you won't sound just like someone else, just as you can't have the same fingerprint as someone else. You're unique and what could be better or more satisfying than finding your own natural sound? Every singing star performing today wouldn't be there if they sounded just like someone else. They had to explore and develop their own strengths, talents and individual sound, just as you will.

Who Should Use This Book

This book is intended for anyone who would like to sing. It may be used by those who never had a lesson and who wish to sing for their own enjoyment; by students who have a limited amount of study; or by those who want to refresh their knowledge of vocal technique. You do not even have to know how to read music to benefit from this book. Perhaps you just want to sing with a Karaoke machine. Students of all styles of singing, from rock bands to church choirs, can use this book to become better, more knowledgeable singers. The vocal technique taught consists of basic principles which apply to all types of singing. If you want to build a house, start with a strong, solid foundation, then build the style of house you desire on top of that. Likewise, if you want to sing, this book will supply you with the information you need to build your own strong foundation in vocal technique that may be applied to any style of singing.

In using this book, start at the beginning, no matter how simple it seems. Do not skip anything, learning each step thoroughly, repeating exercises until you are ready to continue. The success of each lesson is dependent upon the student's understanding and implementation of the information that has been presented previously.

Equipment

The singer's best tool is a notebook or journal. The notebook will allow the student to record his or her observations of the learning process. When something works that helps you in your singing, write it down in the notebook in your own words. Describe what the sensation was like, and what you did to achieve it. This way, you can develop your own troubleshooting checklist. Then, when you experience problems, you can go through your checklist to help pinpoint what it is you are forgetting to do—or not to do.

The student is directed to use a mirror in specific exercises in this book, for observing the movements of the tongue and mouth, and checking vowel positions while singing. Since no one is truly able to hear the sound of their own singing voice as others hear it, a tape recorder is an excellent tool for a singer. The tape recorder will allow the singer to record him or herself singing the exercises and then play them back. When doing this, the student's job is to be an impartial detective, noticing and evaluating everything going on. Do not be too critical at this stage by overengaging in self-evaluation. New tones will not always sound pleasing to the ear. Think of it as an opportunity to listen and objectively correct problems, not as a time to be judgmental. The student should record him or herself singing some of the early lessons and save the tape for later comparison. It is often difficult to note progress in oneself, and this tape will help students hear their own vocal development.

If one is available, a piano or keyboard instrument is very helpful for matching pitches; however, a pitch pipe or other musical instrument can fulfill this role.

Practicing

Improving the singing voice takes a willingness to experiment and the discipline to practice what we learn. It takes time to build new habit patterns in the body. For that is what we are doing: taking old habits that are nonproductive and replacing them with new patterns which are more useful to the student as a singer. In order to produce healthy, vital tones, singers must develop all the factors associated with their singing; for example, the vocal cords, breath, the posture of the body and so on, into a coordinated mechanism that sings. With concentration and determination it is possible to change these habits. However, this coordination may only be achieved through the steady use and practice of the voice, similar to achieving the strength and agility gained from a regular exercise program.

When we practice, we frequently make discoveries about ourselves. It may be helpful to think of practicing as exploring. Exploring highlights the creativity inherent in a successful practice regimen. The best place to do your exploring is a quiet room away from distractions where you feel free to experiment. Sing at a comfortable volume, taking care that it is not so loud that it strains the very muscles we are seeking to train or so soft that full benefit cannot be gained from the exercises. Also, for all vocal practicing, a standing position is preferable due to its positive influence on energy and correct posture.

The exercises should be repeated until the student is satisfied with the results. That is to say, until the student is easily able to sing the exercise at the correct tempo with no straining or tension, and accomplish the goals of the exercise. At this point, the student may move on but should retain the mastered exercises in the practice regimen.

A beginning student should practice no longer than 15 to 20 minutes at a time but may engage in more than one practice session a day. The reasoning behind this is that the exercises demand total concentration in order to effectively build new habit patterns, and after 15 or 20 minutes, the average student's concentration begins to wane. It is recommended that the student take a break at this point and resume after a few minutes or later in the day.

Try to stay relaxed during practice sessions, but if there are any signs of vocal stress or pain, stop the session immediately. When this occurs, to continue vocalizing would only reinforce bad habits, and it is best to stop and resume singing at a later time.

Voice training is a journey of psychological as well as physical development. Struggles are inevitable, but without them, no true progress can be made. If you keep working at it, you will be continually improving each day, sometimes in subtle ways, sometimes in monumental ways. The point is, a musician's technique continually evolves, and each day you will be a little better than you were the previous day. The voice is part of a living, changing organism, and as such is never stagnant.

Vocal Health

Singers cannot remove their instrument and place it in a case for safekeeping when they are not using it. A singer's instrument is the body, and it is affected by all aspects of the singer's life. Hydrating the vocal cords by drinking plenty of water helps to keep them in good working order. Lack of sleep will show up in the voice and can contribute to a fatigued sound. Even excessive coughing, clearing the throat and sneezing can be harmful by placing a sudden strain on the vocal cords. Smoking causes the membranes of the vocal cords to swell, resulting in poor vocal production and clarity. If one stops smoking, a clearer tone and general vocal improvement can be noted within a few weeks. A healthy body is one step toward achieving a healthy voice.

Important!

Teach Yourself to Sing may be used without the aid of a teacher. However, if you are interested in learning more about singing, working with a private voice teacher is highly recommended. A good teacher will recognize and correct problems in a student's singing in a quick and efficient manner, guiding the student's progress and saving much time and frustration.

Acknowledgments

I am grateful to Morton Manus who gave this project special care and attention and to Iris Manus who helped it all come together. Thanks to the entire Alfred team particularly Link Harnsberger, John O'Reilly, Kim O'Reilly, Rob Wren, Ron Manus and Bruce Goldes. Lasting thanks to my students and teachers, especially Peggy Norcross, my friend and mentor. Much gratitude to friends Lucy Ewell and Gwen Bailey-Harbour, and finally to my parents and family, with loving thanks to my husband, Andrew.

About the Recording

 Track 1

Companion recordings are included, which offer practice exercises and song accompaniments. The track number on the recording corresponds with the track numbers listed throughout the book. In using the exercises, although they may have a limited amount of repetitions, the student is encouraged to continue the patterns upward through the comfortable vocal range. Play Track 1 now.

HOW TO READ MUSIC

Although it is true that some singers do not read music, this skill will only enhance one's range as a performer. If only in the area of choosing music (being able to tell "how it goes"), the ability to read music is definitely an asset. You may already be aware that as the notes on the staff travel upward, the sounding pitches get higher, and as the notes on the staff descend, the sounding pitches get lower. This chapter will give you some of the tools you need in order to function in the musical world.

Music is a language all its own and, just like learning any other language, requires some study and effort. However, once you have learned the language of music, it will be an asset to you. When it comes to understanding the ideas of other musicians and communicating yours to them, knowledge about music and how it is written will only be an advantage.

The idea of being able to write symbols which represent music, an art which is transitory and elusive, is an amazing concept. However, a system that has been developed and in use for centuries communicates musical ideas through the written page quite well.

The Musical Staff

The musical staff is made up of five horizontal lines. Notes are placed on the lines and in the spaces between them to represent the pitches to be sung or played. The vertical lines divide the staff into sections and are called bar lines. The areas between the bar lines are called measures.

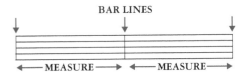

Clefs

Most vocal music is written using one of two musical clef signs. The treble clef 𝄞 is used mostly for notes in higher ranges, and the bass clef 𝄢 (pronounced "base") which is used mostly for notes in the lower ranges. Clefs help to organize the notes into an easily readable format. Most popular and standard vocal copies available in music stores have the vocal line written in the treble clef.

The Names of the Notes on the Staff

Musical notes are named in a repeating fashion utilizing the first seven letters of the alphabet, A to G. In the treble clef the notes placed on the lines are, from bottom to top, E, G, B, D, F (the saying "Every Good Boy Does Fine" is commonly used to remember the names of these notes), and the names of the notes in the spaces spell out F, A, C, E. The line notes in the bass clef are, from bottom to top, G, B, D, F, A ("Good Boys Do Fine Always"), and the spaces are A, C, E, G ("All Cows Eat Grass").

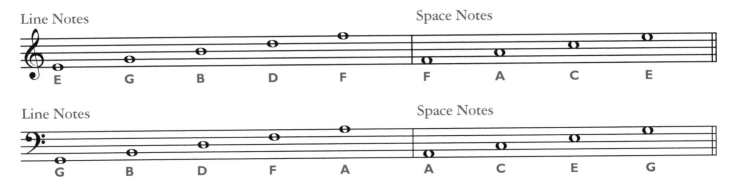

The Names of the Notes on the Grand Staff

A line through a note, a LEGER (pronounced ledger) LINE, is used to extend the range of a staff either up or down as necessary.

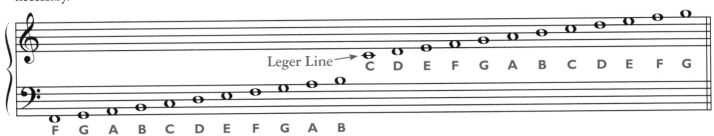

Flats ♭, Sharps ♯ and Naturals ♮

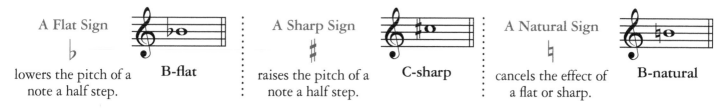

A Flat Sign ♭	A Sharp Sign ♯	A Natural Sign ♮
lowers the pitch of a note a half step. **B-flat**	raises the pitch of a note a half step. **C-sharp**	cancels the effect of a flat or sharp. **B-natural**

The Major Scale

The major scale is comprised of eight consecutive tones in alphabetical order, from "do" to "do" one octave higher.

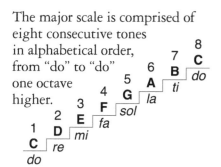

If we start at C and go up the keyboard playing the white notes, we see that all of the tones in the C scale are separated by a whole step with the exception of E to F and B to C, which are half steps.

The pattern of whole and half steps that we saw in the key of C, is the same for any major scale, no matter which note you start on. If, for example, we started on the note G, the scale would look like this:

You can see that the note F has been changed to F♯.

Key Signatures

To make the writing process easier, we can indicate the flats or sharps to be used in a composition at the beginning of the piece. This is called a **KEY SIGNATURE** and tells the performer that the accidentals (flats and sharps) indicated are in effect throughout the piece.

For example the F♯ in this key signature, which appears on the top line of the staff immediately following the clef, indicates that all of the F's in this composition are to be played F♯.

Key Signature of G Major

The Circle of Fifths

The Circle of Fifths is useful for memorizing the number of sharps or flats in a key signature and the order in which the flats or sharps occur, as well as the relationship of one key to another.

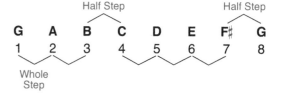

Start with the key of C major at the top of the circle and move CLOCKWISE. Each key is a 5th HIGHER than the previous key and adds one *SHARP* to the key signature. To easily memorize the order of the sharps say

Fat Cats Go Down Alleys Eating Bread.

Again, start with the key of C Major, but move *COUNTERCLOCKWISE*. Each key is a 5th LOWER than the previous key and adds one *FLAT* to the key signature. To memorize the order of flats, just spell **B E A D**, then add **G C F**.

There are TWELVE MAJOR keys. Notice that the last three keys for both sharps and flats are labeled as ENHARMONIC KEYS. The term *ENHARMONIC* is used to describe keys (or notes) that are written differently, yet sound the same. (The key of G♭ sounds exactly the same as the key of F♯.)

THE SYMBOLS FOR RHYTHM

Now that we know how to read the pitches, we also need to know how fast the notes are in relation to the beat. This is the function of rhythm.

Quarter notes ♩ are equal to 1 count or beat. Speak the syllable "ta" to help you count quarter notes.

Half notes ♩ are equal to 2 counts. Say "ta-ah" to count these notes.

Whole notes o are equal to four counts. Say "ta-ah-ah-ah" for counting purposes.

8th notes ♪ are equal to one-half count. Use the syllable "ti" to help count these notes.

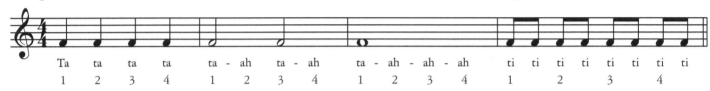

Sixteenth notes ♪ are equal to one-quarter count each. Say the syllables "ti-ri" to help count these.

Dotted notes are notes that are followed by a dot. The dot means that the note value is equal to the original value of the note plus half again. For example: dotted half note = half note (2 beats) + 1 beat = 3 beats.

The Silences

Silences in music, called rests, are just as important as the sounds, because the two accentuate each other. Rests have durations equal to the values of the equivalent note symbols. Therefore, a quarter rest has one beat of silence, a half rest gets two beats of silence, a whole rest has four, and so on. Count the rests silently. It may help to think of the syllable "sh" on each beat.

Time Signatures

The time signature, or meter, of a musical piece is represented by the stacked numbers after the clef sign. The top number tells the musician the number of beats in each measure. The bottom number tells which type of rhythmic pulse gets one beat. 4/4 time means that there are four beats in each measure and the quarter note gets one beat—or in other words, there is the rhythmic equivalent of four quarter notes in each measure.

The Tie

A tie is a curved line that connects two notes of the *same pitch*. A tie is necessary if you wish to hold a note beyond the bar line. Sing the first note and hold it for the combined count of two notes.

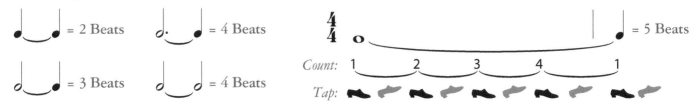

NOTE-READING EXERCISES

Identify the following notes and write their names in the spaces provided below.

1. The notes on the lines:

2. The notes in the spaces:

3. The notes in order:

4. In random order: What do they spell?

4. Answers: DAD, EGG, CAB, GAD, FEED, BED.

PART II—THE BASICS OF SINGING

Breathing

Strangely enough, one of the least understood and commonly overcomplicated parts of singing is the act of breathing. It would seem that we should all be experts at this, having been required to practice it for the majority of our lives. Unfortunately, it is not quite so simple.

Proper breathing is extremely important in singing, because the breath being exhaled works with the vocal cords to create the tone. Correct breathing utilizes the muscles in the lower abdominal region and allows the voice to gain its strength, agility and finesse from this area, taking the pressure off the throat muscles. This allows your true, clear, natural voice to be produced. Since the abdominal muscles are proportionately larger and stronger than the delicate throat muscles, it makes a lot of sense to allow them to do the heavy work.

All of this makes up a natural approach to breathing for singing. Your body already knows how to do it. All you have to do is relax and cooperate. The deep, relaxed intake of air before a sigh is the feeling that you want to have when you take in your breath. The intake of air should activate muscles all the way to the lower abdominal region.

The normal breathing process begins when the brain sends a message to the respiratory system that oxygen is required. The *diaphragm*, a large, dome-shaped layer of muscle which separates the abdominal cavity from the chest cavity, is positioned just under the lungs and aids them in the breathing process. Upon inhalation, the diaphragm lowers, and the rib muscles lift the rib cage. This enlarges the chest cavity, creating a vacuum in the lungs, which expand as they fill with air. Then on exhalation, the diaphragm repositions itself, and the rib muscles relax, aiding the lungs in pushing out the air. Thankfully, the diaphragm is an involuntary muscle or we'd have to spend all of our time trying to remember to breathe!

When air is taken in through the mouth or nose, it travels down the windpipe or *trachea*. The trachea divides at the lungs into two *bronchi*, one for each lung (see diagram), which branch out again 15 or 20 times forming thousands of tiny *bronchioles*.

The lungs are made up of spongy tissue. Their main purpose is to provide the blood with oxygen upon

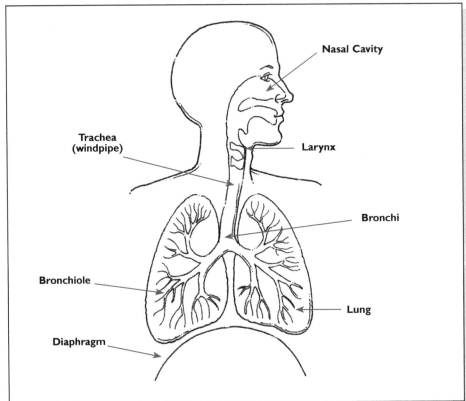

▼ *Respiratory system.*

Nasal Cavity

Trachea (windpipe)

Larynx

Bronchi

Bronchiole

Lung

Diaphragm

inhalation and relieve it of carbon dioxide at the time of exhalation.

It is very important that the throat be a relaxed, open channel through which the air can flow unencumbered. If one has a tight throat, the air will not be able to function freely and can cause vocal distress.

A very calming exercise is for the singer to quietly become aware of his or her breathing. Take a few moments and focus on the breathing process and your body. Take a deep, medium-sized breath and do not allow your shoulders to rise as you draw the breath. Shoulders should stay in a relaxed position, down and back,

resting into the body, thus opening up the chest area. It is necessary for the chest to remain comfortably high and open for optimal lung expansion. When singing, this posture should be maintained throughout the inhalation and exhalation process so that the air is not pushed out of the lungs prematurely and the amount of air sent to the vocal cords may be regulated.

Trying to control the breathing muscles is counterproductive. The extra tension exerted in the body will affect the vocal cords, causing them to tense and strain. Conscious manipulation of the breathing process is truly unnecessary, because the abdominal muscles and diaphragm will naturally work together to regulate airflow. To achieve this, stand tall with good posture. Do not allow the chest to collapse, keep it comfortable, but high. When done properly, these breathing elements will do their job *for* you.

A huge gulp of air does not help you to sing better; conversely, it invites tension. Just as anything in excess tends to be detrimental, too much air often causes rigidity and tension in the throat, and in the lower abdominal region. The key is to sip

Physical Exercises

Most people do not need special exercises to strengthen their breathing muscles. The muscles involved are generally in good shape to function

low, quick breaths in rapid succession. The abdominal muscles will move in and out with each breath. Do this for short stints only, or you will hyperventilate.

3. Exhaling little puffs of air through the nose will also engage the diaphragm. Do about 30 puffs, rest and then do 30 more, increasing

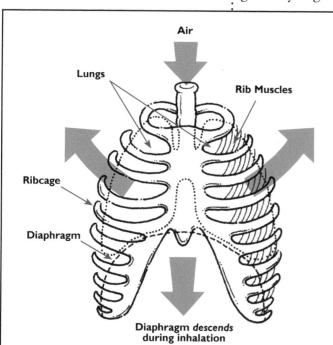

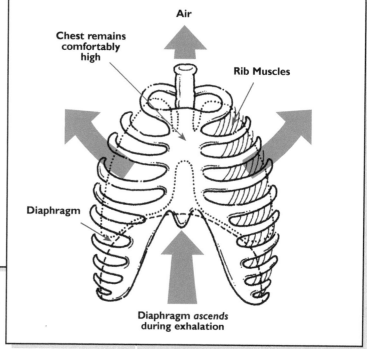

Inhalation during singing

Exhalation during singing

the air. You will be surprised how far a small amount will take you. Just try it and you'll see.

Usually the fear of taking an inadequate breath comes from a feeling of mental insecurity, not an actual physical shortfall. In a deep breathing process such as is used in singing, even though we may exhale a large quantity of air, a good amount of residual air remains in the lungs which generally goes unused. Take heart in the knowledge that you really do have enough reserve available. Trust your body to breathe for you.

> Strive to allow the body to create a balance between the action of the breathing muscles and the amout of air inhaled for singing

for your singing needs. Often, however, there is a lack of awareness of how the body operates.

1. To experience a natural breathing style, lie flat on your back on the floor and just breathe. The body really does know how to do this by itself. We can learn a lot by observing its technique. When we are on our backs we naturally breathe deeply and the diaphragm gets a full workout. Watch your stomach go up and down, relax and listen to your body. The great thing is that if anyone asks, you can tell them you are practicing. This is serious, strenuous work! Don't rush, give it several minutes, and when you feel you understand it, slowly stand up and see if you can recreate the experience from a standing position.

2. Panting is a good way to experience the action of the diaphragm muscles. Inhale and exhale several

the speed. Staying relaxed will enable you to draw in small amounts of air between puffs.

4. The "Rag Doll" is an excellent exercise for allowing the air to act correctly on the inhalation process. To do this exercise, bend over from the waist and allow the upper half of the body to hang loosely like a rag doll. Allow the muscles to completely relax and take some deep, relaxing breaths. After a minute or two of this, slowly stand up. As you rise, try to imagine that you are stacking each vertebra of the back on top of the previous one in a straight line. The shoulders should fall back into place, and the head should come up last. Take a deep breath. Repeat this exercise, and before beginning to stand up, release all your breath. Don't breathe in again until you are in a fully upright position. Take several breaths while you are standing in this position, getting used to

the feeling. The breath should naturally be full, and you will automatically use the muscles in the lower abdomen.

5. From a standing position, remember the feeling of taking in a breath for a sigh, and feel as if the breath is descending to the lowest part of your abdomen. You have to let go of your stomach muscles (there's no room for vanity here) and let them act on their own. You may feel as if your stomach expands out during the inhalation process. This is the diaphragm moving down as you inhale. It is natural and correct.

Upon exhalation, maintain an upright posture and slowly expel the air. You may feel the abdominal muscles moving inward a bit. This is not something that you should help with, the body can take care of it just fine. Place your hands on your abdomen and monitor the movement of the muscles. Repeat 10 times. When you are able to allow the body to take over and move smoothly on its own, an even singing tone is possible.

6. Draw in a gentle, low and full breath to a count of three. Stand about two feet away from a wall, facing it. Exhale the air slowly in a controlled hiss. The throat should be relaxed, acting only as a passageway for the air. Try to maintain an even intensity in the hiss, and imagine that the power of the quiet, steady energy contained in the hiss will slowly push back the wall. Extend the hiss as long as possible, then repeat.

7. Breath control involves developing both agility and flexibility in the muscles used for the breathing process. The action of the diaphragm and lungs can be felt in one's back, so place your hands on your back at the waist level. Imagine that you are a cylinder filling up with air. Breathe deeply and feel your back expand as you fill the area under your hands. Complete, full breathing should include this area of the back.

▼ *Muscle action during breathing*

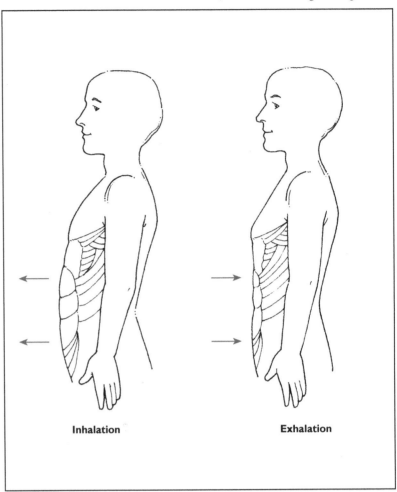

Inhalation   Exhalation

Vocalizing

One of the best ways for singers to build better singing technique is through vocalization exercises. Vocalization exercises are designed to help condition the vocal cords and improve the range and flexibility of the vocal mechanism. You might want to think of them as vocal aerobics.

Warming Up the Voice

It is always a good idea to "warm up" before singing. Singers of all musical styles, from rock to opera, employ vocal warm-up exercises to get their voices moving through their entire range, protect themselves from vocal strain and to prepare for the rigors of performing. Vocal exercises warm up the voice just like stretching movements warm up the body before running or other physical exertion. As with other types of exercises for the body, vocally, it is best to begin gently.

Vowels

Because vocalists sing words and want these to be understood, a lot of time is spent perfecting the way they sing vowels. The tongue and mouth form the vowel shape, and the breath flows through the vocal cords into the mouth. This creates the vowel sounds which we recognize as:

Ah	as in "father"
Ay	as in "say"
Ee	as in "beet"
Eh	as in "red"
I	as in "tie"
Oh	as in "so"
Oo	as in "loom"

Vowels which are made up of two sounds, such as "I" (Ah + Ee) and "Ay" (Eh + Ee) are called diphthongs. The second sound in each diphthong, known as the vanish, should never be emphasized. The vanish is only lightly articulated just as the sound fades away.

In the case of a word containing an "Uh" sound, such as love, dove, because, or the "Ow" sound as in

the words round, down, town, the preferred pronunciation for singing is to slightly modify the vowel toward the "Ah" sound, creating a rounder, more open tone.

The best way to examine and practice the shape required for vowels is to whisper each one. To practice using the "Ah" vowel, whisper "Hah." Feel where the tip of the tongue is, what the sides and back of the tongue are doing. The tongue should be relaxed, with the tip touching the back of the bottom teeth as you whisper the word. Memorize the way it feels.

Singing is based on speech, so after we investigate the feeling of the vowels by whispering, the next step is to speak them. With the jaw relaxed, and the upper and lower back molars slightly apart, very gently say "Hah." Everything in the mouth should remain still. Repeat "Hah" several times, experiencing the sensation of stillness. Whisper "Mm." Still relaxing the jaw, and with space in the mouth, gently say "Mm." On the "Mm" there should be a feeling of vibration in the mouth, but the tongue remains still. This is the beginning of a hum.

Now, try something called the *Speech-Chant*. Combine the two sounds above, saying "Hah-Mm," prolonging the sound, allowing two beats for the "Hah" part and three beats for the

Tony Bennett's clear singing style allows the lyrics to stand out.
▼ (Sony Music/Columbia.)

"Mm" part. Sustaining the sound as if chanting, keep the tone going through the entire five-beat duration of the "Hah-Mm." Make sure that there is space between the back teeth. Repeat "Hah-Mm," not allowing it to die out prematurely. Your desire to communicate prolongs the sound.

> Singing is essentially sustained speech

▲ *Natalie Cole is noted for her careful attention to the words of her songs.* (Photo: Firooz Zahedi. Courtesy of Elektra Entertainment.)

Exercises

All exercises in this book should be sung starting with the notes shown and then progressively raising the notes in the exercise by a half step on each repetition. For example, an exercise which begins on the note C will progress to start on the note C#, then in the next repetition, D, D#, and so on. Continue to sing as high a pitch as is comfortable. Do exercise the upper ranges of your voice and encourage it to grow, but do not attempt to sing the exercises when you are experiencing vocal strain. The number of each exercise refers to the number of the musical example below.

1. Keeping the same gentle, no-pressure feeling used for the Speech-Chant, sing "Hah-Mm," sustaining it on the given pitch. Keep feeding the breath into the tone, maintaining a smooth exhalation.

2. The very tiny distance between the notes in this exercise has a massage-like effect on the vocal cords, making it an excellent way to start the warm-up process. Whisper the vowels, be very sensitive and note the minute movements inside the mouth. Begin slowly, then do the exercise several times, varying the *tempo* (or speed). Start with "Ah" the first time you sing the exercise, then "O." Finally combine the sound as "Ah-O."

3. This exercise uses the humming sound "Mm." The lips are together, but the back molars should be slightly apart. Keep the space open in the throat. The tone should be placed in the mouth; try aiming the sound at the lips. Be careful not to allow it to become too nasal. Keep a consistent energy level.

4. Whisper the vowel first, then sing the exercise. Try to match the vowel on each note to the vowel preceding it.

5. No singing, please! Just speak this one on pitch, saying the numbers.

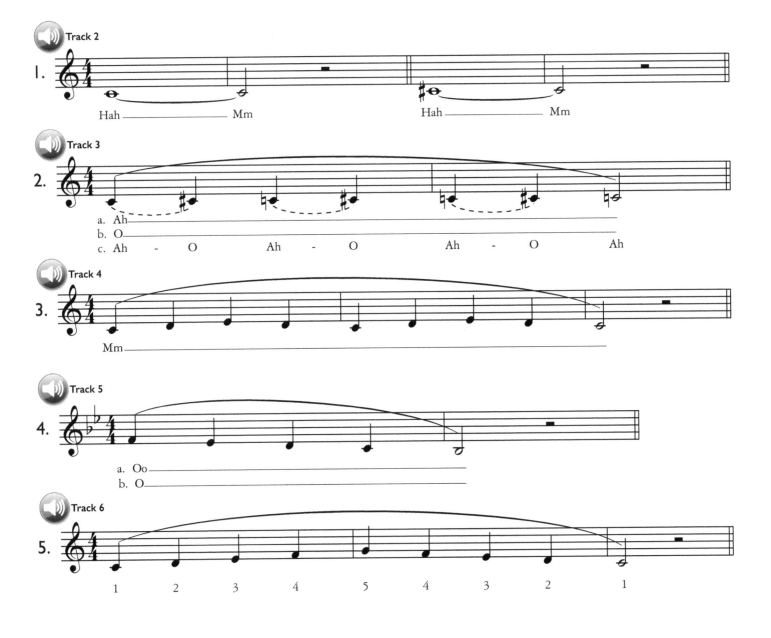

First, just say the words to these folk songs, then sing them on pitch in the same simple way you spoke them.

Slur: ⌒ or ⌣

SLURS mean to sing legato.

LEGATO means SMOOTHLY CONNCTED

Oh, How Lovely Is the Evening Track 7

Traditional Round

Oh, how love - ly is the eve - ning, is the eve - ning,

When the bells are sweet - ly ring - ing, sweet - ly ring - ing,

Ding, dong, ding, dong, ding, dong.

All Through the Night Track 8

Welsh

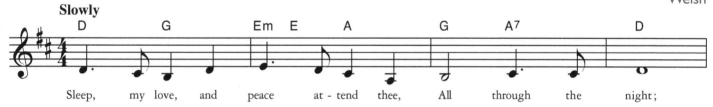

Sleep, my love, and peace at - tend thee, All through the night;

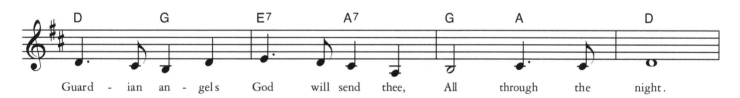

Guard - ian an - gels God will send thee, All through the night.

Soft the drow - sy hours are creep - ing, Hill and vale in slum - ber steep - ing,

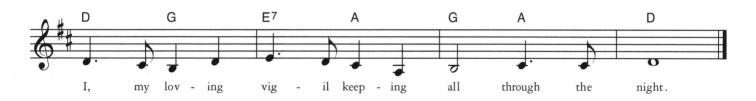

I, my lov - ing vig - il keep - ing all through the night.

Singing Posture

Just like mother always said, good posture is important in presenting yourself to the world—and for good singing, too. A correct alignment of the body is very important to singers, as it helps them to manage their breathing more easily, thus making it easier to produce good singing tones. The goal is to achieve an upright posture that is relaxed and open so that your breath flows in and out of the body as effortlessly as possible. This helps the body manage the breathing process by being aligned instead of bent, just as a straight straw is easier to sip through than a crooked one. This is also important because incorrect posture induces tension, and any tension in the body is easily transmitted to the vocal mechanism and may cause vocal strain.

In building good posture, there are several elements which require attention. First, the feet should

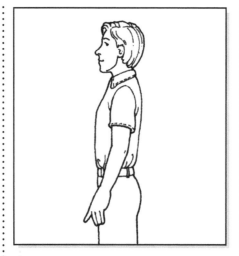

▲ *Good posture*

be planted firmly on the floor, approximately a shoulder's width apart. Imagine that your stance is drawing stability and strength from the center of the earth itself. Knees are relaxed, never locked. Locking the knees reduces blood circulation and you could find yourself in an embarrassing position (face down on the floor) if you attempt to do

this while singing. The spine is as straight as possible—but not rigid, shoulders are down and back—but *relaxed*. Keep a watchful eye on the shoulders as they may have a tendency to creep up around the ears. This is neither an aid to the singing process nor is it a particularly attractive look.

The chest should be open to allow for full expansion of the lungs, the arms hanging loosely at the sides with elbows relaxed and slightly bent. It is also very important to try to alleviate any tension in the neck area, both front and back, as this may cause constriction in the region of the throat. There is a comfortable uprightness to this posture.

A singer's posture is flexible but stable, allowing the vocal mechanism to function freely.

Exercises

It is a good idea to always loosen up and warm up the body prior to singing. Any stretching or limbering exercises can be useful to help prepare the body for singing. Here are some that are particularly helpful for vocal students.

1. To check your body alignment, put your back to a wall and place your feet in a parallel position on a level floor, about two inches from the wall. Bending the knees a bit, place your shoulder blades and buttocks against the wall. Inhale a low breath. Upon exhalation, keeping your shoulders and buttocks against the wall, straighten the legs and lengthen the torso area. The neck and jaw should remain in alignment with the rest of the body, not jutting forward or back. This exercise aligns the shoulders, drawing them back and down, lifts the upper chest and brings the pelvis into position. Take some slow, gentle breaths. Your breathing should be easier, flowing smoothly in and out of the body.

2. Suppose that you were just given extremely good news. Your shoulders go back, the head lifts and the chest fills. Imagine that there is a very long string which attaches your sternum (breastbone) to a star. You feel taller than you think you are. Walk about and enjoy your new found height.

3. The "Rag Doll" exercise previously described on page 9 is not only a guide for the breathing process but releases tension and helps to build an erect posture. After performing this exercise, your body should be in an optimal position for singing. Repeat this exercise several times.

4. Balance Points: For this exercise, stand in front of a full-length mirror. Viewing the body from the side, study the alignment of your overall posture. Now we are going to examine balance points in the body. First, the feet: rock back and forth until you find just the right balance, leaning neither too far over the toes nor back on the heels. Using the mirror as your guide, experiment until you find the right, comfortable place. Next, find the balance point of the hips, moving them back and forth until you find a good midpoint upon which to build the spine. Now, align the shoulders above the hips in the same fashion. Lastly, check the position of the head, experimenting by moving it forward and back until you find the balanced placement. Ears should be aligned with the shoulders and the chin should be level, not tucked down or stretched too high. Now examine the whole effect, take some breaths and try to get used to this new way of standing. Try to maintain the posture as you walk around the room. Repeat daily until you are able to incorporate it into your everyday life; you will seem stronger and more confident.

The Tongue

All the components of the vocal mechanism must be balanced so that they are allowed to function freely without interference from unwanted tension. The tongue is essential to a singer for articulation purposes, but since the tongue often harbors tension which interferes with singing freely, it must be trained to lie relaxed and still in the bottom of the mouth.

> The tongue should be free of tension during singing.

Exercises

1. While observing your tongue in a mirror, silently count to 5 without the tongue moving. The tongue should feel relaxed, fat and low in the mouth. Let go of any residual tension in the shoulders and jaw. Repeat this exercise until the tongue is able to be relaxed and still. Everything inside the mouth should remain motionless. This requires patience and relaxation.

2. Whisper "Ah" with a fat, still tongue. Watching in a mirror, whisper the "Ah" until you can say the vowel without any rippling or other reaction from the tongue.

3. Say "Ah" with a fat, still tongue. Say the vowel for one second, then two, and when you are able to do that without any tongue interference, say it for three seconds and so on, until you are able to maintain a motionless tongue for at least five seconds at a time.

4. Singing is sustained speech. From speech, comes the singing. Sing "Ah" on a comfortable pitch in the same easy way you spoke it. Repeat until the tongue is able to remain motionless in the bottom of the mouth during singing.

5. and 6. Sing the exercises below. The tongue is at rest.

7. Whisper "Ah," then "O." The vowel change should be made with as little movement as possible inside the mouth.

Track 9

5.
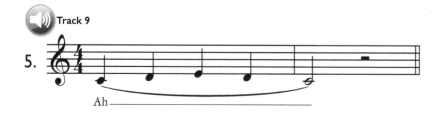
Ah

Track 10

6.

O

Track 11

7.

Ah   O

First just speak the words without being concerned about pitch, then sing the songs on the correct pitches. Be very aware of saying pure vowels as you sing them.

MINI MUSIC LESSON

D.C. al Fine or *Da Capo al Fine:*
This sign indicates to go back to the beginning and sing to the *Fine* (end) *sign*.

All Night, All Day Track 12

Spiritual

All night, all_____ day, An - gels watch - ing o - ver

me, my Lord. _____ All night,

all_____ day, An - gels watch - ing o - ver me.

Now I lay me down _____ to sleep, An - gels watch - ing o - ver

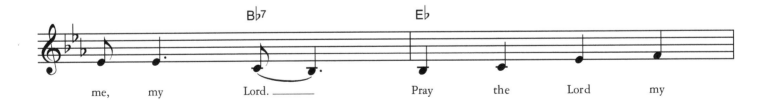

me, my Lord. _____ Pray the Lord my

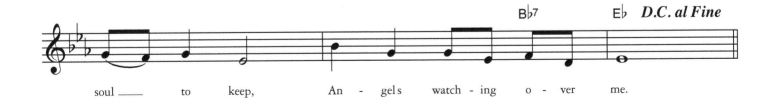

soul _____ to keep, An - gels watch - ing o - ver me.

> **MINI MUSIC LESSON**
>
> ### Incomplete Measures
>
> Not every piece of music begins on the first beat. Music sometimes begins with an incomplete measure, called the UPBEAT or PICKUP. If the upbeat is one beat, the last measure will sometimes have only three beats in 4/4, or two beats in 3/4 to make up for the extra beat at the beginning.

Home on the Range Track 13

American

The Jaw

From the neck up a singer's muscles should be fairly loose and relaxed. This includes the jaw. A tight jaw will limit your ability to sing freely. The jaw is needed for articulation purposes in singing, but even then must be utilized in a relaxed manner.

As one sings higher, the jaw naturally lowers. The idea is to lower the jaw in a way that will result in increased space for the tone, and actually help the singer.

If the jaw is lowered at the point of the chin, the only extra space gained is at the front of the mouth. Opening the mouth in this way may also result in tension in the jaw area. The most beneficial method of opening the mouth for singing is to lower the jaw from the back, at the hinge, around the molar area. This opens up the proper areas that provide the singer with the extra room that they can use. It also places much less strain on the jaw.

To loosen up the jaw area, open the mouth and allow the jaw to hang loosely from the hinge. This is sometimes referred to as a "dumb" jaw. Remember, you are getting used to a new, relaxed feeling and during the exercises in this section, relaxation is far more important than a precise articulation of the words. While singing, try for as little movement of the jaw area as possible. Allow the tongue and lips to do their jobs in pronouncing the vowels and consonants. Check your progress by observing yourself in a mirror and placing your index finger lightly on the chin.

> A relaxed jaw is essential for good singing.

 **Exercises**

1. Experience a feeling of letting go in the jaw and cheeks while you sing this exercise.

2. Sing this exercise with a relaxed jaw, letting it go and allowing your tongue to do all the work. The jaw absolutely does not need to move in order to sing these exercises—make sure there is no chewing of the jaw as you sing! Remember to sustain the tone between the notes and keep singing a pure vowel throughout the exercise.

3. Let go of the jaw and sing the exercise.

4. Use very little movement of the jaw in this exercise. Be very aware of singing a good "Ah." Don't allow this vowel to become "Uh.'"

5. Allow the tongue to work independently from the jaw in this exercise.

Repeat Signs

‖: :‖

The repeat sign indicates that the section of music between the double bars is to be repeated.

Aura Lee

Track 19

Words by W.W. Fosdick
Music by George R. Poulton

Relax the jaw and enjoy the vowels in this lovely folk song.

Kum Bah Yah

Track 20

Spiritual

Singing Vowels and Consonants

Singing could be defined as the act of vocally sustaining a series of vowel sounds which are interrupted by the articulation of short consonant sounds. The vocal channel must be open in order to produce vowels. One of the basic rules of singing is that only the vowels are sung.

Consonants, which are formed by using various combinations of the lips, teeth, tongue and soft palate, interrupt the flow of the tone. Consonants are simply "flicked" off the tongue to make way for the next vowel. Sing the vowel all the way through the note, without allowing the consonants to interfere. In singing a word on two notes like

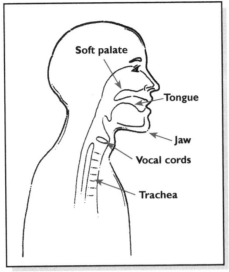

va-lley, pretend that there are two words, "va" and "lley." Don't allow the "va" to migrate to or become tainted by the "l" sound before it

is time to sing the second note on "lley." Try to sustain a note on the "l" or any other consonant and you will understand the difficulties and problems that arise from singing a consonant. The tone is interrupted and closed off. The singer's rule is keep the consonant out of the tone until the very last moment, then immediately go on to the next vowel.

> Singing is comprised of sustained vowel sounds which are briefly interrupted by short consonant sounds.

 **Exercises**

1. The desire to communicate governs singing. This exercise utilizes the idea of "the call," the instance where one might call out to a neighbor or friend when there is a good distance between you, perhaps across the street.

2. Employ the chant in exercise 2. Relax the jaw and feel the vibrations resonate in the mouth and head.

3, 4 and 5. Gently whisper the vowels in these exercises, then say the words. Decide what vowel should be sung for each note. Now sing the exercises slowly, taking care to sing only the vowels; the consonants are very short.

Track 21

1. Hel - lo!

2. Hel - lo, how are you to - day?

Track 22

3. Val - ley, _____ sal - ly.

Track 23

4. Sing - ing, Tra——— La la Tra——— La.

Track 24

5. Glo - ry, lor - ry, lil - y, dil - ly, cho - ral, lau - rel, sor - rel.

Speak the words to the songs that follow, giving special attention to the vowels, then sing them.

Greensleeves Track 25

Moderately *English*

Em G D Em

A - las, my love, ___ you do me wrong ___ to cast me off ___ dis-

Bm Em G D Bm

cour - teous - ly, And I have lov - ed you so long, ___ de-

Em B⁷ Em G

light - ing in ___ your com - pan - y. Green - sleeves ___ was

D Bm Em Bm

all my joy, ___ Green - sleeves ___ was my de - light,

G D Bm Em B⁷ Em

Green - sleeves was my hear t of gold ___ and who but my la - dy Green - sleeves?

Long Time Ago Track 26

American

Slowly

G C G D⁷

1. On the lake wher e droop'd the wil - low long time a - go,
2. Dwelt a maid be - lov'd and cher - ish'd by high and ___ low,
3. Rock and tree and flow - ing wa - ter long time a - go,

C Am G D⁷ G

Where the rock threw back the bil - low bright - er than snow.
But with au - tumn leaf she per - ish'd long ___ time a - go.
Bird and bee and blos - som taught her love's ___ spell to know.

Matching Pitches

Many people believe they can't sing because of an inability to accurately match musical pitches using their singing voices. However, it is very possible to develop one's skills in this area. Excluding medical problems such as cases of severe hearing loss, it is rare to find a person who is completely unable to perceive pitch differences at any level. Most people who have difficulties with pitch were never brought to an awareness of how to really listen and attempt to match musical pitches.

Singers must be aware of the pitches they sing, because it is very difficult to listen to a singer who is sharp (above the pitch) or flat (below the pitch) on any given note. A beginning singer may have mastered a certain style but not be able to match pitches consistently, resulting in "off-key" singing. Singers do not have any buttons to push down on their instruments to help with singing in tune, so they must rely on their ears to guide them. Never "make" pitches from the throat. The singer's thought is what creates the pitch, so *think* the tones.

Sound is vibration which is detected by our ears. The faster the vibration, the higher the pitch. As the vibration slows, the pitch lowers. The note to which most orchestras tune is A above middle C. This note requires 440 vibrations per second (called hertz) to be produced. An octave below that, only 220 hertz are required to produce the lower note A.

> Concentration and focus are essential parts of all singing, but are especially crucial to the pitch-matching process.

Track 27

Exercises

1. Listen to the two pitches played by a piano on the recording or have a friend test you. Are you able to identify the one that is a higher pitch? You may feel that the sounds of the tones evoke different qualities, such as one tone feeling "faster," (higher) another tone feeling "darker" or "brighter." Take note of these ideas, for your perceptions may be very useful to you in identifying pitch differences. (The first note on the recording is higher.)

2. a. Play or listen to the song "Merrily We Roll Along," on the recording. Do you recognize the tune? See page 23.

   b. Sometimes a student has difficulty matching pitches with a piano, but is able to match the pitch of another singer. Have a friend sing or listen to the singer on the recording as she sings the song once. Then repeat the song and sing along with the singer. Record yourself doing this, so that you can check your pitch accuracy. At this point, we are only concerned with the ability to match the pitch, so please do not be critical of the quality of sound. A singer's sound always seems different to them when recorded and played back, but this is a good way for singers to hear their true vocal sound.

   c. This time sing the song alone, matching pitches with a piano or the recording. Record yourself and check your progress.

   d. Record yourself singing the song alone, without any sort of accompaniment. Are you able to make the tune recognizable?

   e. Inner hearing, the ability to hear the notes of a song inside one's head, is a good skill to develop. In this exercise, listen to the recording or have a friend play "Merrily We Roll Along" while you sing the song *inside your head*, not making a sound. This requires a great deal of concentration. Once you are successful at hearing the song while the piano is playing, try hearing it all the way through without the piano.

   You can practice the principles in exercise 2 using other short, simple songs such as "Row, Row, Row Your Boat" or "Mary Had A Little Lamb." Are you able to hear the tunes in your head? If you are not immediately successful at these exercises, keep working at them. Improvement will come with careful practice.

3. This exercise requires the first three tones of a major scale to be spoken on pitch.

4. Speak this exercise on pitch. The pitches are the first five tones of a major scale. Sing this exercise:
   a. with the piano; b. alone; c. inside your head.

5. Sing the 5-tone scale aloud as usual, but leave out the number "3." Sing this number inside your head. Example: "1, 2, _, 4, 5," then omit it again as you descend, "5, 4, _, 2, 1." Experiment, leaving out a different scale tone.

Track 28 Merrily We Roll Along

2. Mer - ri - ly we roll a - long, roll a - long, roll a - long,

Mer - ri - ly we roll a - long, o'er the deep blue sea.

3.
1 2 3 2 1

Track 29

4.
1 2 3 4 5 4 3 2 1

5.
1 2 ___ 4 5 4 ___ 2 1

Play the notes or listen to the recording of each of the following songs. Then when you are sure you know each tune, sing them. Imagine that each note is a bull's-eye, and hit the mark directly in the center of the pitch every time from the first instant you sing the tone. It is easy to get into a habit of always singing the notes in a "scooping" manner—sliding up or down to the pitch. Too much of this effect is annoying to the listener and can be a difficult habit to break.

Go, Tell It on the Mountain   Track 30

Spiritual

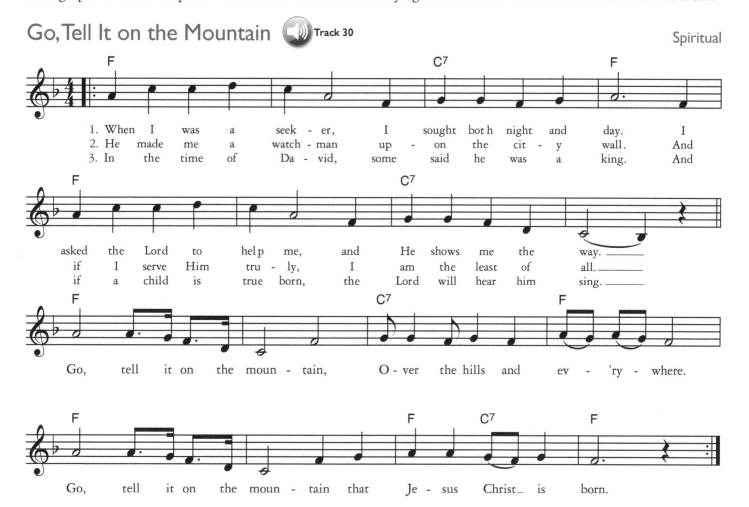

1. When I was a seek - er, I sought both night and day. I
2. He made me a watch - man up - on the cit - y wall. And
3. In the time of Da - vid, some said he was a king. And

asked the Lord to help me, and He shows me the way. _____
if I serve Him tru - ly, I am the least of all. _____
if a child is true born, the Lord will hear him sing. _____

Go, tell it on the moun - tain, O - ver the hills and ev - 'ry - where.

Go, tell it on the moun - tain that Je - sus Christ_ is born.

The Fermata

The fermata signifies a hold or pause. The note is to be held longer than the normal duration of the note.

Flow Gently, Sweet Afton Track 31

Words by Robert Burns
Music by James E. Spilman

Flow gent - ly, sweet — Af - ton a - mong thy green braes ; Flow

gent - ly, I'll sing thee a song in thy praise; My Ma - ry's a -

sleep by thy mur - mur - ing stream, Flow gent - ly, sweet Af - ton, dis -

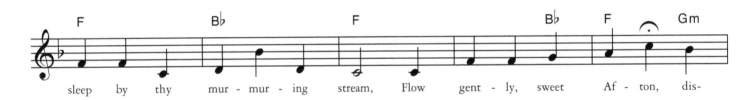

turb not her dream. Thou — stock - dove, whose ech - o re - sounds from the

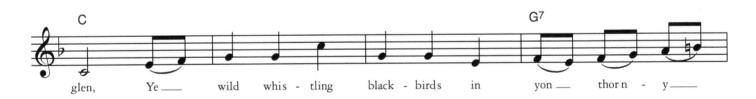

glen, Ye — wild whis - tling black - birds in yon — thorn - y —

den, Thou green - crest - ed — lap - wing, thy scream - ing for -

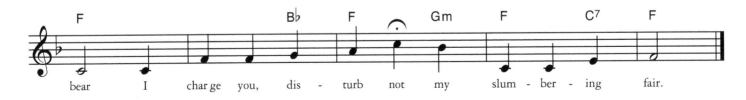

bear I char ge you, dis - turb not my slum - ber - ing fair.

The following two songs will give you the chance to show off all the new skills that you've learned. Use your best posture, breathe low to support the tone, relax the jaw and sing the vowels. Have fun! Elvis Presley recorded a best-selling version of this song—see page 42.

Are You Lonesome Tonight?  Track 32

Words and Music by
Roy Turk and Lou Handman

A rousing rendition of this song was recorded by Peter, Paul and Mary—see page 28.

see page 28.

Cut Time ₵

MINI MUSIC LESSON

The symbol ₵ means "cut time," that is, the time value is cut in half: the half notes receive 1 beat, the quarter notes receive ½ of a beat, etc. **C** or "common time" stands for a time signature of 4/4.

This Land Is Your Land

Track 33

Words and Music by Woody Guthrie

PART III—MORE BASICS OF SINGING

Learning to sing is a cumulative process. The student should aim to master each new technical element as it is introduced and add it to their vocal technique. All of the factors introduced thus far need to be included in your singing. This includes correct posture, breathing and keeping the jaw and throat relaxed.

Vocal Space

Having enough space available for the tone inside the mouth is vital to good singing. When singers describe their singing as having "space" or being "open," they mean that everything is relaxed and free in the column of the throat and in the mouth. The feeling of a yawn is a great way to experience this. The beginning of a yawn allows us to feel the space inside the mouth and throat. The jaw is relaxed, and it is as if there is a large, imaginary orange in the back of the mouth. The space is flexible, never rigid. Be careful that the tongue doesn't pull back into the yawn space. It should lay low and still in the mouth. The space occurs without the tongue's help or interference.

There must be energy in that space as well. It is the energy that is present when you take in a breath for a phrase of music; it has a purpose and it has space. The singer's intent (the intention to sing a phrase of music) provides the energy.

> The singing tone must be surrounded by space.

 **Exercises**

1. and 2. Maintaining the space described above, say Ah! as an exclamation, as if someone just surprised you in the most amazing way. Put the surprise into your eyes as well and say the vowels in the same manner. Now sing the exercises through your eyes, keeping surprise and the element of wonder in your voice. Remember to keep the feel of a yawn in the back of your mouth.

3. Sing the word "Sigh" with a yawning feeling. Provide the space in the upper jaw, but aim the tone at the front teeth.

4. Before singing, whisper "O," then "Oo," noting the tiny differences between these vowels. The vowel "Oo" feels like a smaller vowel; however, the space inside the mouth remains the same as the "O." Simply use the lips to say "Oo."

5. For this exercise, let go of the lower jaw and keep saying the vowel. Laugh your way through this exercise as if you had just heard a delightful story.

Peter, Paul and Mary's tight vocal harmonies and universal ▶
audience appeal make their folk-style songs very enjoyable.
(Photo courtesy of Peter, Paul and Mary.)

Relax the jaw, check posture and provide
the following songs with a lot of "yawn"
space around the tone.

The Water Is Wide Track 38

English

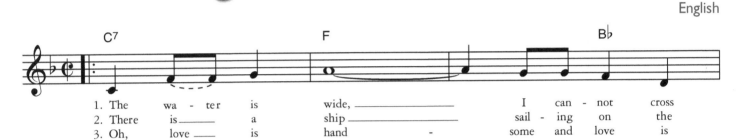

1. The   wa – ter   is   wide, _____   I can – not cross
2. There is ___ a   ship _____   sail – ing on the
3. Oh,   love ___ is   hand -   some and love is

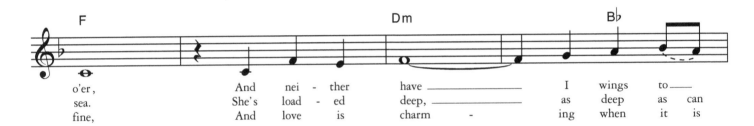

o'er,   And nei – ther have _____   I wings to ___
sea.   She's load – ed deep, _____   as deep as can
fine,   And love is charm -   ing when it is

fly.   Oh, go and get _____
be.   But not so deep _____
true,   As it grows old -

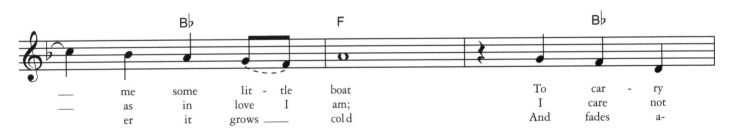

___ me some lit – tle boat   To car – ry
___ as in love I am;   I care not
___ er it grows ___ cold   And fades a-

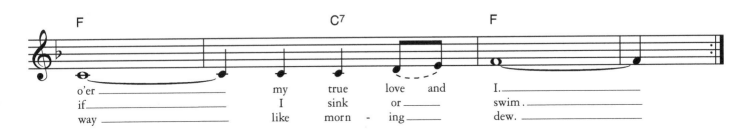

o'er _____ my true love and I. _____
if _____   I sink or swim. _____
way _____ like morn – ing _____ dew.

The Riddle Song  Track 39

English

```
            F                                      Bb
1. I     gave     my     love     a      cher  -  ry     that
(2.) can    there     be      a      cher  -  ry     that
(3.) cher  -  ry   when   it's    bloom  -  ing,     it
```

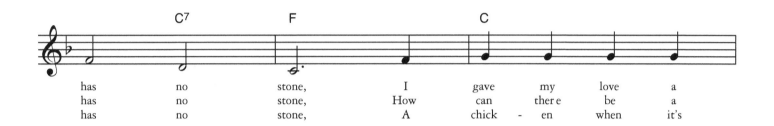

```
        C7           F                C
has     no     stone,     I     gave     my     love     a
has     no     stone,     How   can     there   be      a
has     no     stone,     A     chick  -  en    when    it's
```

```
    F           Dm              Am                  C
chick  -  en         that     has     no     bone,        I
chick  -  en         that     has     no     bone,        How
pip  -  ping,        it       has     no     bone,        A
```

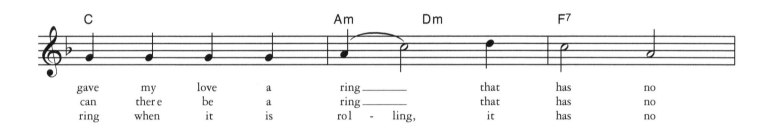

```
    C                       Am         Dm           F7
gave     my     love     a      ring_____     that     has     no
can     there   be      a      ring_____     that     has     no
ring    when    it      is     rol  -  ling,    it      has     no
```

```
    Bb6                    F                       Bb
end,       I     gave     my     love     a      ba  -  by   with
end,       How   can     there   be      a      ba  -  by   with
end,       A     ba  -  by    when    it's    sleep  -  ing,   there's
```

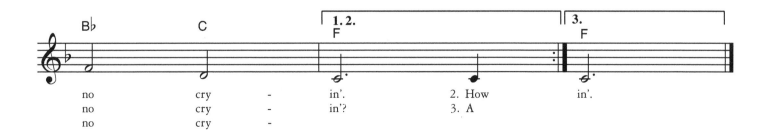

```
    Bb           C        | 1. 2.          || 3.
                          |  F             ||  F
no      cry  -  in'.          2. How          in'.
no      cry  -  in'?         3. A
no      cry  -
```

Energy

Energy, motion and rhythm are central to life. There is rhythm and energy in our sense of time, the seasons of the year, night and day, the tides, even within our own bodies, represented by our heartbeat.

A good singer is able to incorporate energy into a song and maintain it at a consistently high level while engaging in the act of singing. When performing, the singer must be absolutely overflowing with energy even while still or silent. The energy that a singer maintains is primarily mental. It is a combination of concentration, excitement, awareness and intent. The tone must be constantly refreshed with that energy at each new note.

It helps to visualize movement to create energy in your singing. Take a little walk around the room. If you think "1 - 2 - 3 - 4" as you walk at an easy pace, you physically feel movement. Add the words of a simple song like "Twinkle, Twinkle, Little Star," and walk to the tempo of the music. There is energy present, even in this children's song. Now, imagine that you are in a grand parade and sing the song in this style, marching to the beat. The energy will be different in the song, and subsequently your body energy will change to match it.

Music is a great source of energy and movement. The tempo, rhythm and vitality of the music serve as inspiration for the singer's energy. The emotion contained in the music also provides great impetus for the singer. Ideally, the singer will be motivated to synchronize his or her energy with the energy and excitement contained in the music. This is inherent in all successful singing.

> The musical energy of tempo, rhythm, emotion and movement all inspire the singer's energy.

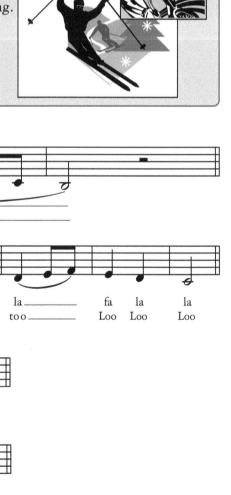

Exercises

Imagine movement as you sing the exercises below. In your mind's eye, see yourself skating, skiing or cycling through the phrase. Substitute your own meaningful image to keep the energy in the phrase moving. Which image creates the most vitality in your singing? Try several and decide which idea works best for you.

1. Say the vowel and keep the music flowing in this exercise.

2. Even passages which contain little musical motion must be infused with energy. Experiment to discover an image that will help you keep the momentum going.

3. Allow this exercise to bubble over with the energy of laughter.

4. Sing this exercise smoothly. Take a breath at the comma above the staff.

5. Experiment with movement to this exercise. Dance it.

Track 40

1.
a. E_____ Ay_____
b. Ah_____ O_____

Slowly

2.
a. Ah _____
b. O _____

3.
a. Fa ____ la____ fa la la
b. Loo ____ too____ Loo Loo Loo

Track 41

4.
Nah_____ Nah_____

Track 42

5.
a. Ah _____
b. O _____
c. Now __ is the time to sing __ and play.

Each song in this chapter has a different kind of energy. Sing the songs using the motion image(s) that work best for you.

MINI MUSIC LESSON

ritardando or *rit.* indicates a gradual slowing down of the tempo or speed.

poco rit.: Slowing the tempo a little.

a tempo: Return to the original tempo.

Simple Gifts Track 43

Scarborough Fair Track 44

More Breathing Strategies

We have already discussed the basics of breathing for singing. Now we come to the singer's eternal concerns: What is the proper amount of air to inhale in preparation for singing any given phrase of music? How much do we really need? Of course, the correct response to these questions is, "Enough." How do we know what "enough" is? Well, the answer is that we don't. The good news is that our body does know and we need to learn to trust its judgment.

Notice your breathing right now. The body is taking care of everything. We don't have to think "Okay, breathe now, out, in, out, in." We couldn't handle it! The body regulates the amount of air it needs. It's the expert, so let it do its job. Our singing isn't helped when we draw in too much air and hold it, then press it out of our lungs. Overinflating like this can cause physical problems, vocal strain and pitch problems. Even when encountering the longest phrases, try taking just a small amount of air before you sing. The best singing results from simply breathing in order to stay alive and allowing the body to do the rest. The real issue isn't how much air is taken, but how naturally it is received and what happens after the breath is inhaled. The intake is very easy. You really use very little breath when you sing. When it is time to make a tone, all that is required is the thought and the body will see to it that there is an adequate amount of air to sing through the music. The singer takes the breath, opens up the channel for the air and then allows the body to take over. There is cooperation. It's like riding a roller coaster and instead of fighting the ups and downs, settling in and going with it as a friend. There is a partnership of the mind and body, not a power struggle.

> The mind and body work together to provide the right amount of air for singing

Exercises 1 and 2. Take in your breath as if you were able to draw in the air through every pore in your face. Sing the "Ah" as in the word "father." Relax the jaw, provide the open space in the mouth and drop into the "Ah," as if you are dunking a tea bag. It is a feeling of resting into the body, not a forced, upward motion.

3, 4 and 5. First speak the words to these exercises. Try different inflections in your voice: happy, sad, questioning, authoritative. Now sing the exercises, starting from speech. Keep it simple—speak them on pitch.

Determine the inflection you want to use with the following songs. With a feeling of resting into the body, sip the air and sing!

Drink to Me Only with Thine Eyes   Track 47

English

The Band Played On   Track 48

Words by John E. Palmer
Music by Charles B. Ward

Vocal Resonance

Resonance is defined as intensifying and prolonging a sound. Of course, we use resonance every day when we speak, otherwise no one could hear or understand us. The vocal cords begin the tone by vibrating using breath expelled by the lungs. Next, the sound is intensified and modified by the resonators. The throat, mouth and facial bones are the primary resonators for the voice. Singers generally focus on two types of resonance used in singing: chest resonance (chest voice) and head resonance (head voice).

Chest resonance can be felt by placing a hand on the breastbone (sternum) and singing a note in one's lowest register. You should feel a vibration in the chest area. As you can see from this experiment, our bodies work much like the body of an instrument, a violin for example, by providing a resonating chamber for the tone.

Head resonance may be sensed by humming a tone in the upper range of the voice. Head resonance mainly utilizes the bone structure in the front of the face and other areas inside the head to conduct its vibrations.

Beginners tend to use vocal tones which are either purely head resonance or chest resonance. The goal is to achieve a blend of these resonances, always having some mixture of the two in varying amounts, depending on the pitch.

As you can see from the resonance diagram, when the voice is in the lower range, most of the resonance should be in the chest, with just a little head resonance present. Ideally, as the notes get higher, the chest resonance becomes less and head resonance increases, ultimately reaching the very highest range of the voice, which should use mostly head resonance with very little chest voice present.

> Ideally, the singing voice is a mixture of the head and chest resonances in varying degrees, depending upon the pitch.

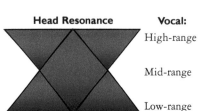

Head Resonance   Vocal:
High-range

Mid-range

Low-range
Chest Resonance

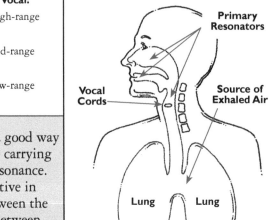

Primary Resonators

Vocal Cords

Source of Exhaled Air

Lung   Lung

Exercises

1. The hum is a good way to experience carrying power and resonance. Be very sensitive in order to experience how the voice is able to manage the balance between the two resonances. Sing this exercise slowly and allow the movement between the notes to be very smooth. This exercise will also require a good, low breath, meaning one which utilizes the lower abdominal muscles.

2. Experience the feel of a yawn. As you sing the exercise, feel the yawn space, and relax the jaw.

3. Before singing, draw your breath in preparation for the highest note in the phrase, and sing the vowels.

4 and 5. Keep saying the vowel in these exercises. The quality of each vowel should match the quality of the first vowel.

Track 49

1. Mm

2.
a. Fa la, fa la, fa la, fa la, la
b. Oo - loo, oo - loo, oo - loo, oo - loo, oo
c. Ea - sy, ea - sy, ea - sy, ea - sy, ee

Track 50

3. The road is low.

4.
a. Ah
b. O

5.
a. Ah
b. O
c. Oo

Hum the first line of each song before singing. Feel the resonance and then sing into it.

Fear of Flying–or–Approaching "Higher" Pitches

Many people feel nervous as they approach pitches in music which seem "high" to them. This is a common reaction, but happily, there are several very effective ways of dealing with this fear of heights.

The first step when one encounters any sort of vocal difficulty with a phrase of music should be to check that the best posture is being used, with the chest high and open, and that you are sipping in a low, deep breath and allowing the jaw to be loose with plenty of space inside the mouth.

Next, a singer should always examine the vowel. Take the time to identify exactly what the vowel is for each note and make sure you are saying it in the best possible, tension-free way. It is often permissible for vowels on high notes to be modified to an easier, more open vowel. Often, a modification toward "Ah" is substituted if it is close to the original vowel and the word may still be understood. Experiment and find a vowel you can sing easily that doesn't distort the word and substitute that instead of the original, offensive vowel. If the singer sings the new vowel and thinks the original vowel, then the word will be communicated to the audience.

Sing the phrase on the vowels only, leaving out the consonants altogether. Then, when you feel you have mastered it and are singing the right vowels in the correct manner, put the consonants back in and see if you can now sing the phrase with more ease. Try this technique on the first line of the song "Row, Row, Row Your Boat." By removing the consonants, we discover that the only vowel sung in this phrase is "O." The "O" is interrupted only briefly by consonants, and all that needs to be done here is to say "O." Sing the phrase on the vowels and then add the consonants. This adds a new awareness of the vowels. In the first line of "Twinkle, Twinkle, Little Star," the vowel sounds are "Ih," "Uh," and "Ah." Sing the vowels, then add the consonants. This adds clarity to the vowels.

Make sure your warm-up includes notes which are a good deal higher than the highest note in the piece of music you are about to sing. This way you can be confident that you are able to sing the pitch, and it won't feel so high. The "siren" is a good way to explore the outer reaches of your vocal range. Inhale a low, gentle breath and starting with your lowest comfortable note, imitate a siren on the word "hi" as the notes glissando (slide) upward to a comfortable pitch in your head voice range and then glissando down again. As you get higher, have a lighter feel to the voice. If you are about to climb a mountain, you probably wouldn't want to take along 300 pounds of luggage. Similarly, when you sing the siren, try traveling light. If you can sing the note in the siren, it is available to you for use in a song. Repeat the exercise several times, each time progressively raising the pitch of the highest tone.

If you are still experiencing difficulties, perhaps what you need is a new mind set. Remember, it is the thought process that actually controls vocal production. Referring to notes as "higher" or "lower" is simply a random assignment of terms to these concepts deriving from the way the pitches appear on the musical staff.

Singing is an act of balance and coordination. All the elements used for singing must be coordinated in the way that is most useful to us and balanced so that no one element takes precedence over the others. The concept of balance and coordination in singing particularly applies to high notes. When the notes go up, often a person's natural instinct is to have all their muscles rise with the tones. Soon the singer is perched on tiptoe with their shoulders up around their ears. Contrary to this instinct, the singer should be relaxing into the body and counteracting the upward motion. This is the time to let go and allow the body to do the work.

The very words "high note" or "low note" strike terror in the hearts of some singers. There is no such thing as a high note or low note, so don't let these terms get in the way of your singing.

> The thought process controls vocal production and there is no such thing as a "high" or "low" note.

▲ *Smokey Robinson's effortless high notes characterize his vocal style.*
(Photo courtesy of Motown Records.)

Exercises

1. Explore the ranges of your voice. Using the siren call on "hi," follow the shape of the diagrams below with your voice, moving it according to the direction of the lines.

2 and 3. Imagine a piano keyboard. All the keys are on the same plane. The keys for the "high" pitches aren't higher than the others, they are on the same level with all the rest of the keys, and the same is true for the "lower" pitches. Sing the following exercises and imagine that your singing is taking place on a keyboard.

4. Sing the next exercise and use the image of fishing—cast the line, and the place ahead of you that you cast it to is the so-called "high" note.

5 and 6. In these exercises, try an image of descending to the "high" note. Even though you are approaching the note from below (the reason it seems high), imagine that you are already above the note, so singing it is just a matter of coming down to that pitch. Make sure that you are actively saying the words with a desire to communicate. This will also help with singing a higher pitch.

After you have experimented with each approach, decide which one works best for you, record it in your notebook and tuck it into your bag of tricks so you will have it to help you resolve any future difficulties.

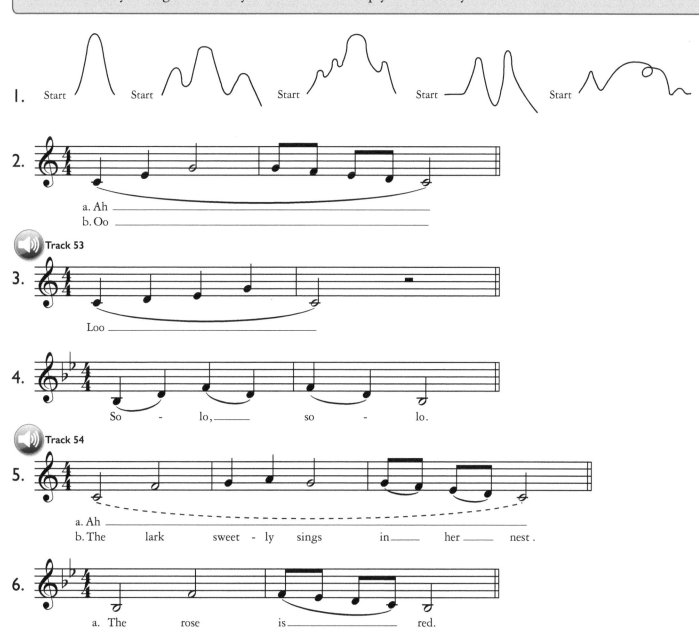

Speak the words and learn the notes thoroughly before singing the following songs so that unexpected pitches do not build tension into your singing. Use your best image for the "faster" pitches.

Amazing Grace  Track 55

Words by John Newton
Music Traditional

Slowly

1. A - maz - ing grace! how sweet the
(2.) Grace that taught my hear t to
(3.) man - y dan - gers toils and

sound, That saved a soul like
fear, And grace my fears re -
snares I have al - read - y

me! I once was
lieved; How pre - cious
come; 'Tis grace hath

lost but now am found, Was
did that grace ap - pear The
brought me safe thus far, And

blind but now I see.
hour I first be - lieved
grace will lead me

2. 'Twas home.
3. Through

Auld Lang Syne 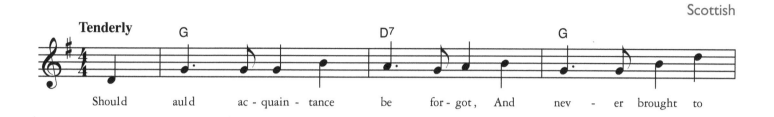 Track 56

Scottish

Should auld ac - quain - tance be for - got, And nev - er brought to

mind? Should auld ac - quain - tance be for - got, And

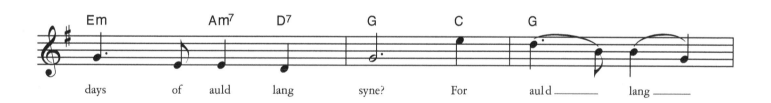

days of auld lang syne? For auld _____ lang _____

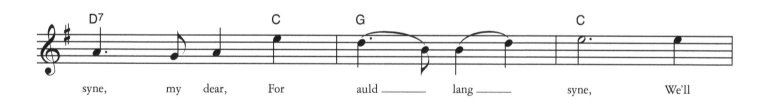

syne, my dear, For auld _____ lang _____ syne, We'll

take a cup o' kind - ness yet for ___ auld _____ lang _____ syne.

Singing for Joy

As we've discussed, singing should be effortless, a walk in the park, but how about fun? During all the "work" that singers do to perfect their voice, they often forget the key elements that attracted them to singing in the first place–the thrill of being alive and the joy, fun and beauty of music.

Please don't forget to include these special ingredients in your singing. Sometimes we get so wrapped up in producing our best tones that we forget that singing is a way of expressing joy. I have seen otherwise beautiful performances marred by a singer's overly serious manner or even the sense that they are just trying too hard. Maybe they are enjoying it underneath but have not

allowed that to show through to the audience. They have forgotten the childlike abandon of dancing, of laughter—they've left out the joy. The point is this: if you aren't finding pleasure in the process of singing, how will others enjoy your singing?

> Singing is a joyful act.

Exercises

The following exercises are "just for fun," so sing away and enjoy!

1. Laughter is a method of communication which carries very well, so laugh your way through exercise 1. It should also be a good workout for the abdominal muscles.

2. Let go and enjoy the freedom in this exercise. Sing it like a stream spilling over stones.

3. Make sure this exercise has the freedom to really dance. Experiment with some movement as you sing it. How does this influence your energy?

4 and 5. Sing these exercises for the pure joy of it.

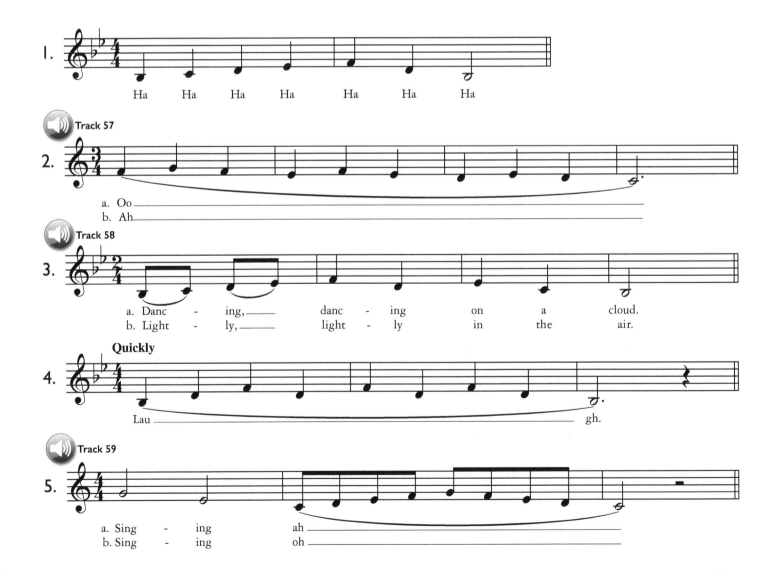

Swing Low, Sweet Chariot  Track 60

Find the joy in each of these songs and allow the notes to bubble up from your most joyous self.

Hopefully

Spiritual

Swing low, sweet char - i - ot,_____ Com - in' for to car - ry me

home; Swing low, sweet char - i - ot,_____ Com - in' for to car - ry me

home. I looked o - ver Jor - dan and what did I see?_____

Com - in' for to car - ry me home; A band _ of an - gels

com - in' af - ter me,_____ Com - in' for to car - ry me home.

Water Come-A Me Eye Track 61

Jamaican

Rhythmically

1. Ev - 'ry time I 'mem - ber Li - za,
2. Since you gone the days are lone - ly,
3. When you here the time goes fast, ___

Wa - ter come - a me eye.

When I think 'bout my gal Li - za,
Come back gal, I love you on - ly,
Now you gone and love is past, ___

Wa - ter come - a me eye.

Come back, Li - za, come back, gal, ___ Wa - ter come - a me eye.

Come back, Li - za, come back, gal, ___ Wa - ter come - a me eye.

Choosing New Music

As your vocal abilities progress and grow, you will want to apply your skills to learning some new songs. You will probably become more aware of songs that you hear and will often consider whether they are appropriate for you to sing. There is an art to choosing suitable vocal music. To aid you in making your choices, here are some of the factors you should consider when "auditioning" a new song.

The first thing to look at when choosing new music is the vocal *range* that the song covers. This means looking at the highest and the lowest notes in the song and evaluating whether the singer has those notes in his or her vocal range and can comfortably sing them.

The next element to consider is the *tessitura*. The tessitura is the place where the song "lies" in the voice, or the range of notes most commonly used in a particular musical composition, not including infrequent high notes or low notes. We might say that the entire vocal range of a piece is an octave, but if it spends most of the song around three or four of the lower notes, then that is the tessitura. If those notes are in the singer's lower vocal range, then we say that the tessitura of that song is low. A singer may be able to handle the range of a particular song, but it is also important to consider whether the tessitura of a song will be a comfortable one for the singer to maintain.

The next factor for consideration is the tempo, or speed, of the song. Do the notes fly by too quickly for the singer to keep the tempo steady, or do they go by so slowly that the singer is in danger of running out of breath before the ends of phrases? Sometimes slight tempo adjustments can be made to accommodate a vocalist, but the tempo marking reflects the character of a song as well as the composer's wishes and should be adhered to as much as possible.

Last, but not least, the lyrics or drama of the song should be considered.

Is it something that the singer has the dramatic range for and will feel comfortable portraying to an audience?

After careful consideration of all the elements listed above, a singer should be able to select music that will show off his or her vocal talents to the greatest advantage.

Learning Songs

Of course, all anyone who picks up a new song wants to do is to sing it. However, there is an art to learning songs well and with the least amount of frustration. The following techniques will help you to learn a song—no matter what the style may be—in the most efficient manner, eliminating the need to relearn a song which has been learned with incorrect elements such as rhythm or pitches.

The first step is to read through the words. Make sure you are familiar with the general meaning or story of the song. This way you can begin to think of the dramatic intent of the song right from the beginning and start to plan how you want to communicate that meaning when you sing.

The next step is to take the time to work out the exact rhythm to the words. Mark the beats in the music if necessary. It is important to learn the rhythms accurately now, because if you do not take the time to do this correctly at the beginning, it will take you a lot more time to "fix" it if you are singing incorrect rhythms. This is also the reason it isn't a good idea to learn a song from a recording. A recording artist may not be completely accurate in their rendition of the song or may prematurely influence you to imitate their style or artistic decisions. Singers should give themselves time to develop their own interpretation of a song and, if possible, not

listen to anyone else do it until they have worked out a pretty good idea of what they want.

If a song's tempo is very fast, work it slowly at first, then gradually increase the speed until you arrive at the correct tempo.

Once you can speak the words in rhythm, do this while you or someone else plays the pitches on the piano. Repeat this step several times until you know what to expect in the music, so that no "high" or "low" notes take you by surprise. After doing this several times, you will know the song without ever singing it. Now that you know it, sing the song, one phrase at a time, slowly working out vowels and articulation. Lastly, sing the entire song. Now that you've learned it, the only work left is to memorize it and work on the dramatic presentation.

Elvis Presley was a genius at selecting music that was perfect for his unique singing style.
▼ (Photoplay Archives/LGI Photo Agency.)

INTERPRETATION PART IV–INTERPRETING VOCAL MUSIC

Learning the notes and the rhythms is really the easy part to performing a song. The more difficult task for many performers lies in the interpretation of it, portraying the drama and soul of a song to an audience.

Telling a story

The point of singing is to use words in conjunction with the music to tell the story of a song. Songs in all styles of music have a story line, and your interpretation can enhance the drama inherent in the song. As with learning the notes and rhythms, the drama in a song is extremely important or the song just won't come across to an audience. After studying the words and determining the meaning of the song, there are several artistic decisions you can now make.

What is the song about?

In five words or less, identify the essential gist of the song. (Examples would be love, unrequited love, joy, sorrow, frustration and so on.) This basic question will help you find the heart of the song and establish it in your mind. Your answer to this question may change or evolve during your association with a song.

What is the mood?

The general mood of a song must be created by the singer. This question is closely tied to, "What is the song about?" The answer to that question will be helpful in determining the overall mood that you wish to convey. The tempo and rhythm of the music will also provide some clues as to the mood. A song with a quick, lively tempo should leave a very different impression on the audience than a slower moving piece. Similarly, examining rhythmic patterns in the song should give you some ideas about how to sing it.

Who is the narrator of the piece?

Develop a personal history of the person. This may be more important in some styles of singing than others, but it can't hurt to know the character. Are they male or female? What is their approximate age? Where are they from? Lastly, in correlation with the mood of the song, what is the narrator's attitude?

Location: Where are they when they are singing?

You will want to consider this question carefully, because whether your narrator is in jail or at a dance will tend to affect your interpretation.

Are they singing to someone or something?

What is their relationship with the person to whom they are singing? How do they feel about this other person (or cat, horse, truck)? These answers will give you some feelings to work with. If the narrator is in love with the person they are singing to, he or she will probably show more tenderness, for example, than they would toward someone or something they dislike. Or, there may be layers of feelings. If the singer is singing about unrequited love, there is probably love toward the object of their affection beneath their hurt and resentment.

Is there humor present?

Humor may be present in an explicit manner in a comedy song, or may only be implied in others. Seeking out the humor in your piece is a positive move for your interpretation and will help you build rapport with the audience.

Not necessarily all of these items will pertain to every song, but careful consideration of them will help you to develop an interpretation. Try out several choices for each question, ranging from the obvious to the surprising. Experiment until you find an interpretation that is interesting and will work for you.

Based on your answers, experiment with the way you should stand, using a full-length mirror to gauge the effect. Try out some gestures, remembering that too many can be distracting. Words that are repeated are usually repeated for a reason. Figure out the reason and find a new way to sing them each time, perhaps through the use of dynamics (loud or soft) or other vocal expression.

Determine your focus. If you are speaking to someone in the song, where is that person—on your right or left, or perhaps directly in front of you? Visualize the events of the song, make up a story for it and see it vividly in your mind, creating a movie in your mind for yourself. Use this to fuel your performance and engage the audience in seeing and feeling the song as strongly as you do.

Each of the songs in this chapter has a different story line and emotion. Visualize the story and sing with that feeling. Keep your excitement and energy working in a positive way for you, maintaining a relaxed and open feeling in the body.

Give My Regards to Broadway Track 62

Words and Music by
George M. Cohan

The Ash Grove  Track 63

Welsh

1. The ash grove how — grace - ful, how plain - ly — 'tis — speak - ing, the wind through — it — play - ing has lan - guage for me; When o - ver its — branch - es the sun - light — is — break - ing, a host of — kind — fac - es is gaz - ing at me. The — friends of — my — child - hood a - gain are — be - fore me, each step wakes — a — mem - 'ry as free - ly I roam. With soft whis - pers — lad - en its leaves rus - tle — o'er me; the ash grove, — the — ash grove that shel - tered my home.

2. My laugh - ter is — o - ver, my step los - es light - ness, old coun - try - side — meas - ures steal soft on my ear; I on - ly re - mem - ber the past and — its bright - ness, the dear ones — I — mourn for a - gain gath - er here. From — out of — the — shad - ows their lov - ing — looks — greet me, and wist - ful - ly — search - ing the leaf - y green dome; I find oth - er — fac - es fond bend - ing — to — greet me; the ash grove, — the — ash grove a - lone is my home.

Musical Expression

To sing well, the muscles in the throat, jaw and mouth should be relaxed and free. This is true since, as we've discussed, the abdominal muscles do the bulk of the work. Some words of caution, however. Singing takes an incredible amount of energy, on a level with that required by an athlete. Don't mistake a lack of energy as the type of relaxation I have described. The challenge for singers is to keep their energy flowing in a productive way and not allow it to manifest itself as tension.

Phrasing

The best way to add expression to singing is to begin with the words. They will tell you how to sing the song. When a singer can say the words convincingly and demonstrate an understanding of the text, then he or she will know how to sing the song. Additionally, clarity of diction is extremely important for singers because the words must be understood.

When the words are separated from the music, they may seem trivial. The performer's job is to find the emotional impetus to justify the music. Practice telling the story in your own words, so that you may gain a thorough understanding of the words and emotions behind them.

> Speak the words with feeling and then sing

Phrasing adds clarity to the lyrics of a song, just as it does to our speech. As in speech, commas, periods and sometimes other punctuation usually imply the end of a phrase. Within reason, if there is a comma or a period in a sentence, that is where the singer may breathe unless the composer has indicated otherwise.

When beginning to work out the phrasing of a song, speak the text and take a breath every place the punctuation indicates. This method of phrasing will probably result in some inappropriate or unnecessary breaths. Of course, a singer must use good judgment and not overindulge in breathing if there are several commas in a sentence. The singer may not need all the breaths they have available to them, or conversely, they may need to seek out a place to breathe when one is not readily available. When singing, just as in speech, one would never breathe in the middle of a word. Speak the phrase you intend, try it out and make sure that the meaning of the words will not be misconstrued in any way by your breathing. Finally, enter in your music all the breaths you have decided upon as commas or check marks above the music. Essentially, breathe where it makes the most sense.

Before singing the following songs, speak the words with feeling and plan your breathing.

Red River Valley Track 64

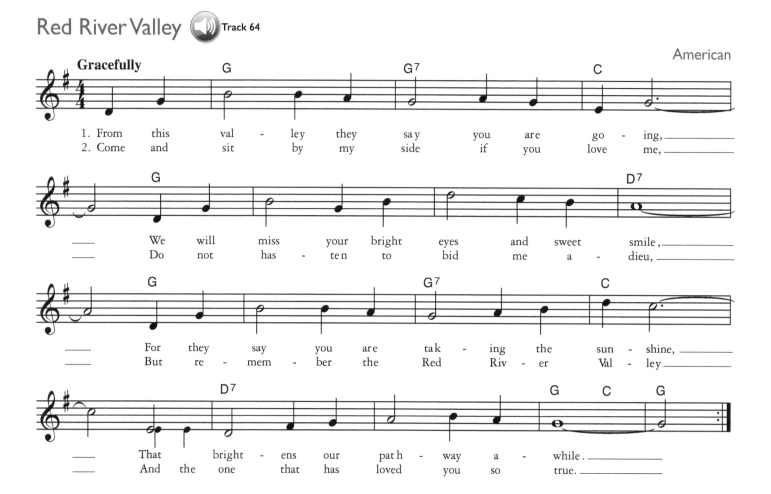

You Made Me Love You  Track 65

Words by Joe McCarthy
Music by James V. Monaco

Dynamics

One of the simplest ways to add more expression to your singing is through the use of dynamics (loud and soft). After you have given some thought to the dramatic intent of a song, you may feel that some passages require more or less volume than others. This contrast will make your presentation more interesting. In some types of music, the composers will indicate in the written musical score what they feel would be an effective dynamic, thus making the singer's job easier. It is still a good idea to experiment and discover the best places in the song for dynamics or special effects that seem to make the most musical sense to you.

For instance, in the case of a repeated phrase, you probably wouldn't want to say it exactly the same way twice. There should be something different about each repetition.

Musical Dynamics

pp	*pianissimo*	very soft
p	*piano*	soft
mp	*mezzo piano*	medium soft
mf	*mezzo forte*	medium loud
f	*forte*	loud
ff	*fortissimo*	very loud

crescendo	increasing in volume
decrescendo	decreasing in volume

It is actually the intent of the singer, inspired by the lyrics of the song, that changes the volume of their singing. The thought that a certain passage should be louder or softer signals the body to make the appropriate adjustments. The singer's energy must remain constant while changing dynamics. A note might be sung softly, but that doesn't mean that the energy should be pulled away from it. Keep feeding the breath into the tone, maintaining a smooth exhalation.

Exercises

1. As when we speak, the intensity of softer phrases does not diminish when we sing. In your normal speaking voice, speak the phrase, "I will do it now." Repeat the phrase at a level of mezzo piano, but still with the intent to communicate. Next say the phrase pianissimo or very softly, but with purpose. Now say it in a louder, firm voice at a level of forte.

2 and 3. Sing these exercises, exploring the dynamic possibilities of your voice.

4. In this exercise change the dynamics as indicated with each phrase.

5. Sing the exercise according to the dynamics indicated.

Follow the dynamic markings and sing with energy throughout.

Legato and Staccato

The techniques of *legato* and *staccato* singing are additional ways to add interest to a song.

Legato is a style of singing which is very smooth and connected. There are no gaps between notes; all the space is filled with lush, fluid sound.

It is notated with a slur over or under the notes.

Staccato style may be likened to a laugh and is notated with a dot over or under the note head. A good, old-fashioned "Ho! Ho! Ho!" is a good example of the detached feel of staccato.

> Legato phrasing requires long, fluid lines, and staccato notes are short and detached.

Exercises

1. Sing this exercise legato, connecting all the notes. To help you envision the kind of fluid connection needed for this style of singing, imagine you are stretching apart a piece of chewing gum.

2. Sing the same exercise, laugh it and keep the notes short and detached.

3. This exercise combines staccato and legato singing.

4 and 5. Sing the exercises as indicated by the phrasing.

This song is an example of soothing legato style.

Down in the Valley  Track 73

American

In this song, the staccato style notes lend a sense of merriment.

Deck the Halls Track 74

English

Interpretive Exercises

Every time you sing, whether it is a song or a vocal exercise, you have an opportunity to develop your interpretive powers. Nothing you sing should be without expression. This way, you get used to including drama and feeling in your singing and not having to toss it in as an afterthought immediately before a performance.

When people speak, they use many types of inflections (happy, sad, etc.) and tone colors to illustrate their speech. Tone color and inflection help us determine the meaning of a person's words. This expressiveness is already a characteristic of speech and is our starting point for integrating it into our singing.

The following exercises are designed to help you to explore your creativity.

Exercises

1. Speak the phrase in the moods indicated, then sing it.

2. Say the word "love" in the moods indicated, then sing it.

3. How do you respond to various colors? Sing these exercises as the colors indicated. Note the ways in which they differ. For example, how does "pink" sound in contrast to "blue"?

4. Sing the colors indicated below.

Track 75

Joyful, sad, puzzled, angry

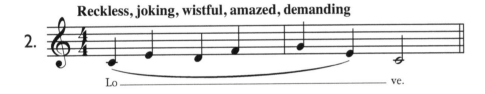

1. Will you — go to - day? _____

Reckless, joking, wistful, amazed, demanding

2. Lo _____ ve.

Track 76

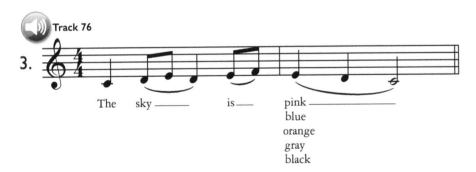

3. The sky _____ is _____ pink _____
blue
orange
gray
black

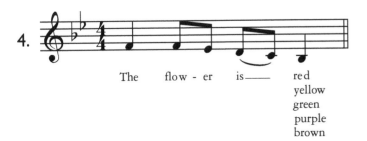

4. The flow - er is _____ red
yellow
green
purple
brown

Musical Styles

Singing a song in an appropriate style is essential to a good performance. Classical music has very strict guidelines governing its performance techniques. Musical theater is somewhat less so, and other styles, such as rock, country, pop or jazz, while still having notable musical characteristics, tend to have a more relaxed approach.

Popular Music

Popular music, which includes the genres of folk, country, rock, pop and jazz, is very relaxed in its interpretation. In these styles, the goal is to be unique and make the presentation as individual as possible. Anything goes as far as stage movement for the popular singer— whatever conveys the message of the song is appropriate. A knowledge of microphone technique is essential to this style. As opposed to the classical singer, the popular singer is permitted to add embellishments to the music at will, or even change the key of the song, raising or lowering it to bring it into a more comfortable range.

Jazz

Jazz style utilizes unusual accent notes on unexpected beats, sudden dynamic changes and various vocal effects, particularly the use of "scat" singing, which imitates instrumental sounds.

Musical Theater

This type of performing demands the portrayal of a dramatic role; therefore, the drama is of equal importance to the vocal expertise. Musical theater singers must be particularly mindful of a healthy singing technique. In their quest to portray a character fully, the danger is to allow a character's vocal idiosyncrasies to interfere with healthful vocal production. One may still portray a character vocally and maintain a healthy technique by employing proper breathing and support.

A musical theater singer is also required to dance and will have free range of the stage in keeping with the character. Songs are sung in the original key and a high level of energy is essential.

Vanessa Williams's sensitive approach to popular music is enhanced by her excellent vocal technique. (Photo: Peter Lindbergh, courtesy of Mercury Records)

Classical Style

In classical vocal music, which includes opera, oratorio, recital and much of the music written for the church, the singer must be able to sing competently in several languages (particularly Italian, French, German and English), act and look good while doing all of it. When singing in a language that the singer is not fluent in, exact pronunciation and diction are extremely important as slight variations in pronunciation may have a great effect on the meaning of the text. The drama in classical vocal music is important. Traditionally, the singer communicates the meaning of the text with very little stage movement.

▲ *Bruce Springsteen's energetic stage presence combined with his own distinctive lyrics create a powerful performance.* (Sony Music/Columbia Records)

The performer's focus and stance can portray a great deal during a song. The song is performed in the original key as written, without embellishment. The classical singer does not generally use a microphone.

Putting It Together

Many new performers tend to be reserved in their interpretations of songs. As you gain more performing experience, you will develop an instinct for what is appropriate for each song. At first, it can be difficult to show that much of your inner self when presenting a song. A way to work on developing an interpretation is to experiment in your early rehearsals. Allow yourself the freedom to try all sorts of things, appropriate and not, overdramatize, stretch yourself. Then, tone it down if necessary, keep what works and discard the rest. Each singer must make a song his or her own, giving it their own unique twist.

> The audience will relate to you if you keep your interpretation simple and let the emotion shine through.

PART V–PERFORMING MUSIC

PERFORMANCE

After a performer has successfully conquered most of his or her vocal difficulties, the culmination of successful voice training is a demonstration of vocal talents through performance. Singing in front of an audience involves believing in yourself and takes courage. To be able to sing well, you must be willing to reveal to the audience your most vulnerable inner self. It requires a certain measure of self-confidence, recklessness and the willingness to take a chance.

Since the whole point of singing is to communicate, singers need to work on communication skills. Surprisingly, a lot of professional performers identify themselves as basically shy people. Yet, onstage, they are outgoing and expansive.

Most singers will be nervous the first few times they perform. A technique that works quite well is to turn negative energy, which is fear, into positive energy, which is excitement. If you can convince yourself that you are excited and eager to perform and that the butterflies you feel inside are generated by excitement, then you will probably have a much more enjoyable performing experience. However, the real remedy for performing anxiety is practice. Just like anything else, the more you do it, the less nervous you will be and the more confident you will become of your skills. Don't allow errors that happen onstage to discourage you. Stay calm, treat them as your teacher and learn from them. The next time you perform, you'll be stronger for having experienced and dealt with them.

While worrying about every nuance, singers occasionally forget that they should just sing. Sometimes, it takes getting the brain out of our way to allow the music to really soar.

Taking the Stage

Walking onto a stage can be one of the most exciting experiences of one's life. It can also be very frightening. Confidence makes the difference. If you don't feel

▲ *The three tenors (l. to r.) Placido Domingo, José Carreras and Luciano Pavarotti are masters at taking and holding command of the stage.* (Photo: The Los Angeles Times.)

confident, try to act like you do. Sometimes just by pretending we are confident, some of that sureness slips into our being and encourages us. Audiences are generally on the side of the performer, wanting them to do well. Everyone knows what it is like to watch someone uncomfortable on stage struggle through their piece. Their unease affects everyone in the audience, which subsequently ends up sharing the agony along with the performer.

Practicing every element of your performance is the best way to gain confidence. Rehearse everything, from start to finish. Practice the way you will walk out onto the stage, all the nuances, gestures and movements during the song, and the way you will accept applause and acknowledge your accompanist or band, and finally how you will

leave the stage. Study your body language in a mirror to make sure you are giving the effect you want. Try standing confidently, as if you "own the stage," and act like you really want to be there. Go over this until you feel comfortable with it. Take it one step farther, and visualize yourself all the way through a successful performance.

Today's technology gives us an advantage over singers from previous generations. Have a friend film or videotape your performance so that you can see yourself as the audience sees you. Study it carefully and make any necessary adjustments.

On the day of the performance, make sure you've warmed up vocally. Some performers find it helpful to also do mental and physical warm-ups prior to a performance. Knowing you are warmed up and have done your preparation will give you some control over the situation and increase your self-assurance on stage. Smiling, making eye contact when

Nat "King" Cole had a warm, personal style of communicating with an audience that made you feel like an old friend. (Institute of Jazz Studies.)

you walk out onstage and treating the audience as welcome guests are also good ways to establish rapport.

When it comes down to actually doing the performance, remember that your job is to transport the audience into the make-believe world of the song. In order to accomplish this, you need to let go and portray the feelings of the song for them. Take a deep breath, go out there, give to the audience and enjoy yourself!

Using a Microphone

A microphone takes the sound waves of your voice and amplifies them, electronically enhancing the volume of your voice as it goes through the speaker. Using a mic can be helpful or even expected in certain performing situations (like pop music or club singing) and you should be aware of ways to use a microphone to enhance your performance.

When using a microphone, sing in your regular voice and don't hold back. However, don't make the microphone do all the work for you. It is a tool to enhance your voice's volume, not a way for the singer to become lazy and slip into bad habits.

Experiment to determine the optimal distance from your mouth to the microphone. The distance will vary depending on the type of microphone being used and the style of music being performed. Rock and pop music may require a closer mic technique than other styles.

If you are using a microphone that has a cord, be very aware of what your hands are doing. Don't play with the cable, it is very distracting. You want the audience to focus on your face and the song, not the hand that is fidgeting with the mic cord. Of all types of microphones, wireless or cordless microphones allow performers the greatest amount of freedom. When using a wireless mic, performers are able to dance and move about on stage without restrictions.

If you plan to use a microphone regularly for your performing, it is advisable to get some practice using one offstage. Do some experimenting to find out the best way a microphone can enhance your performance.

Karaoke

Karaoke is a popular form of entertainment that began in Japan and has spread to other countries around the world. It can be found in many restaurants and night spots and allows singers with all types of experience and backgrounds to perform in front of an audience.

A karaoke machine plays a song which has been prerecorded without the lead vocal line. The performer sings into a microphone that amplifies his or her voice and also mixes the performer's vocals with the instruments and any background singing on the tape.

There are a wide range of songs from which to choose, and an exciting aspect of singing karaoke in a club is the use of a song video which helps portray the mood of the song and has on-screen lyrics for the singer.

One added feature on a karaoke machine is that most can be adjusted for pitch, raising or lowering it as dictated by the singer's needs. So, if your favorite song was always just a bit too high or too low for you to sing comfortably, here is your solution.

A Few Last Words

Once a student has developed good technique, it must be practiced to be maintained. The voice is constantly changing. Maturity as well as vocal training are factors which shape the singing voice and contribute to a person's individual sound. Continue your vocal education by listening to good singers and learning from them.

Music is in the hearts of all people. If singing is in your heart, look at the world with wonder, learn, be joyous, be yourself and incidentally, you will *sing*.

About the Author

Karen Farnum Surmani has several years of experience as a private vocal instructor and delights in working with students of varied backgrounds and ages. She performs frequently as a professional singer. Ms. Farnum Surmani holds a degree in Vocal Performance and a teaching credential in music education. Her vocal studio is in the Los Angeles area.

Turn! Turn! Turn!
(To Everything There Is a Season)

Track 77

Words from the Book of Ecclesiastes
Adaptation and Music by Pete Seeger

Moderately, not too fast

Verses 3 & 4

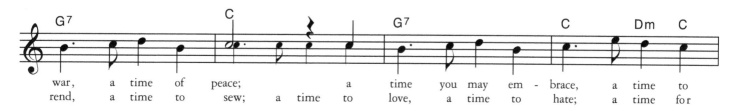

mf
3. A time of love, a time of hate; a time of
4. A time to gain, a time to lose; a time to

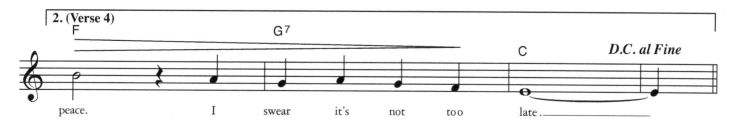

war, a time of peace; a time you may em - brace, a time to
rend, a time to sew; a time to love, a time to hate; a time for

1. (Verse 3)

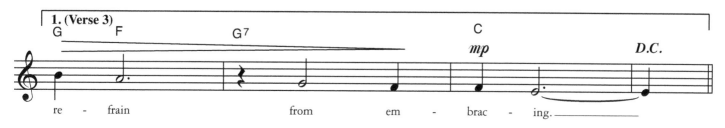

mp   **D.C.**

re - frain from em - brac - ing.

2. (Verse 4)

D.C. al Fine

peace. I swear it's not too late.

▲ *The Byrds are best known for their recording of "Turn, Turn, Turn."* (Photo courtesy of Sony Music.)

Those Were the Days

Track 78

Words and Music by Gene Raskin

◀ *Barbra Streisand's versatile singing style has allowed her to popularize many different types of songs including a moving version of "For All We Know."*
(Photo: Firooz Zahedi)

For All We Know   Track 79

Words by Sam M. Lewis
Music by J. Fred Coots

* **Triplets:** A triplet is a group of three notes played in the space of two notes of the same value.
Triplets are indicated by a "*3*" above or below the note grouping.

The lyrical interpretations and jazz stylings of Frank Sinatra have made him a timeless performer. (Institute of Jazz Studies.)

Fly Me to the Moon
(In Other Woods)
Track 80

Recorded in a Jazz style by Frank Sinatra.

Words and Music by Bart Howard

Slowly and tenderly

Fly me to the moon, and let me play a- mong the stars; Let me see what

spring is like on Ju- pi- ter and Mars. In oth- er words: ___ hold my hand!

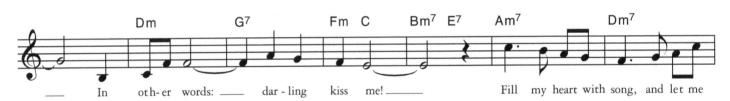

___ In oth- er words: ___ dar- ling kiss me! ___ Fill my heart with song, and let me

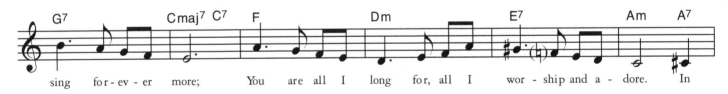

sing for- ev- er more; You are all I long for, all I wor- ship and a- dore. In

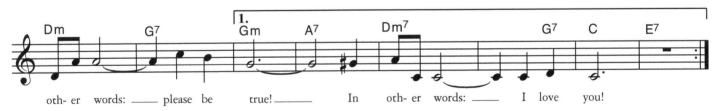

oth- er words: ___ please be true! ___ In oth- er words: ___ I love you!

True! ___ In oth- er words: ___ I love you!

Dream a Little Dream of Me  Track 81

Words by Gus Kahn
Music by Wilbur Schwandt and Fabian Andree

Where Is Love?  Track 82

From the Columbia-Romulus Film *Oliver!*

Words and Music by Lionel Bart

Slowly but rhythmically

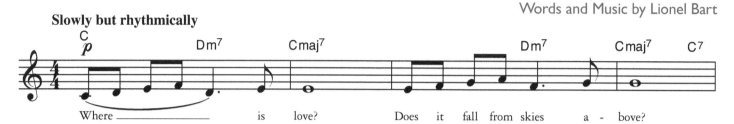

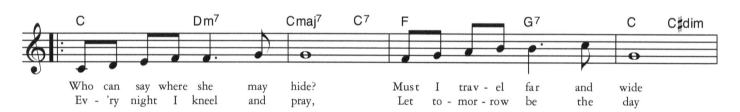

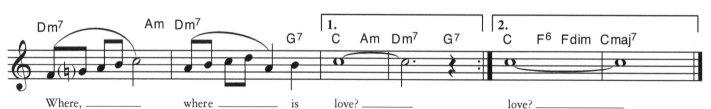

The form of this English Renaissance madrigal is as follows: sing the first section of verse 1 twice, observing the dynamics, *forte* the first time and *piano* the second time. Then sing the second section of the first verse once. Return to the beginning and repeat verses 2 and 3 of both sections in the same way.

Now Is the Month of Maying Track 83

Thomas Morley

1st section

Quickly

1. Now is the month of May - ing, When
2. The spring, clad all in glad - ness, Doth
3. Fie, then, why sit we mus - ing, Sweet

mer - ry lads are play - ing.
laugh at win - ter's sad - ness. } Tra la la la la la
youth's de - light re - fus - ing?

la la la la la, La la la la la la

2nd section

la.

1. Each with his bon - ny
2. And to the bag - pipe's
3. Say, dain - ty nymphs, and

lass A - dan - cing on the
sound, The nymphs tread out their
speak, Shall we play bar - ley

grass, }
ground, } La la la la la,
break? }

Return to the beginning for verses 2 & 3.

La la la la la la la, la, la la la la.

Use these charts to form chords in any key!

Chord Chart

ANY KEY

MAJOR
ROOT 3rd 5th

MINOR
ROOT 3rd 5th
lowered
½ step

DIMINISHED
ROOT 3rd 5th
lowered lowered
½ step ½ step

AUGMENTED
ROOT 3rd 5th
raised
½ step

DOMINANT 7th
(3rd or 5th may be omitted)
ROOT 3rd 5th 7th
lowered
½ step

Major Scale Chart

ROOT	2nd	3rd	4th	5th	6th	7th	8th
A♭	B♭	C	D♭	E♭	F	G	A♭
A	B	C#	D	E	F#	G#	A
B♭	C	D	E♭	F	G	A	B♭
B	C#	D#	E	F#	G#	A#	B
C♭	D♭	E♭	F♭	G♭	A♭	B♭	C♭
C	D	E	F	G	A	B	C
C#	D#	E#	F#	G#	A#	B#	C#
D♭	E♭	F	G♭	A♭	B♭	C	D♭
D	E	F#	G	A	B	C#	D
E♭	F	G	A♭	B♭	C	D	E♭
E	F#	G#	A	B	C#	D#	E
F	G	A	B♭	C	D	E	F
F#	G#	A#	B	C#	D#	E#	F#
G♭	A♭	B♭	C♭	D♭	E♭	F	G♭
G	A	B	C	D	E	F#	G

How to Use the Charts

All chords are formed by combining certain tones of the major scale according to definite rules. For example, any MAJOR CHORD is formed by combining the ROOT, 3rd and 5th tones of the MAJOR SCALE of the same name. The chord may, of course, be inverted by moving the root to the top: 3rd, 5th, ROOT, and again by moving the 3rd to the top: 5th, ROOT, 3rd.

The construction of some chords involves lowering or raising one or more tones ½ step. For example, to form the C DIMINISHED CHORD, look up DIMINISHED in the CHORD CHART on the left, above. Note that the diminished chord consists of a ROOT, a 3rd lowered ½ step, and a 5th lowered ½ step. Look up the C MAJOR SCALE in the chart on the right, above. Note that the ROOT is C, the 3rd is E, and the 5th is G. Since the 3rd and the 5th must be lowered, make each of these FLAT; thus the C DIMINISHED CHORD is C E♭ G♭. The chord may be inverted, of course.